OCE-8   OCCUPATIONAL COMPETENCY EXAM SERIES

This is your
PASSBOOK for...

Building Maintenance

Test Preparation Study Guide
Questions & Answers

COPYRIGHT NOTICE

This book is SOLELY intended for, is sold ONLY to, and its use is RESTRICTED to individual, bona fide applicants or candidates who qualify by virtue of having seriously filed applications for appropriate license, certificate, professional and/or promotional advancement, higher school matriculation, scholarship, or other legitimate requirements of education and/or governmental authorities.

This book is NOT intended for use, class instruction, tutoring, training, duplication, copying, reprinting, excerption, or adaptation, etc., by:

1) Other publishers
2) Proprietors and/or Instructors of "Coaching" and/or Preparatory Courses
3) Personnel and/or Training Divisions of commercial, industrial, and governmental organizations
4) Schools, colleges, or universities and/or their departments and staffs, including teachers and other personnel
5) Testing Agencies or Bureaus
6) Study groups which seek by the purchase of a single volume to copy and/or duplicate and/or adapt this material for use by the group as a whole without having purchased individual volumes for each of the members of the group
7) Et al.

Such persons would be in violation of appropriate Federal and State statutes.

PROVISION OF LICENSING AGREEMENTS – Recognized educational, commercial, industrial, and governmental institutions and organizations, and others legitimately engaged in educational pursuits, including training, testing, and measurement activities, may address request for a licensing agreement to the copyright owners, who will determine whether, and under what conditions, including fees and charges, the materials in this book may be used them. In other words, a licensing facility exists for the legitimate use of the material in this book on other than an individual basis. However, it is asseverated and affirmed here that the material in this book CANNOT be used without the receipt of the express permission of such a licensing agreement from the Publishers. Inquiries re licensing should be addressed to the company, attention rights and permissions department.

All rights reserved, including the right of reproduction in whole or in part, in any form or by any means, electronic or mechanical, including photocopying, recording, or by any information storage and retrieval system, without permission in writing from the Publisher.

Copyright © 2025 by
National Learning Corporation

212 Michael Drive, Syosset, NY 11791
(516) 921-8888 • www.passbooks.com
E-mail: info@passbooks.com

PASSBOOK® SERIES

THE *PASSBOOK® SERIES* has been created to prepare applicants and candidates for the ultimate academic battlefield – the examination room.

At some time in our lives, each and every one of us may be required to take an examination – for validation, matriculation, admission, qualification, registration, certification, or licensure.

Based on the assumption that every applicant or candidate has met the basic formal educational standards, has taken the required number of courses, and read the necessary texts, the *PASSBOOK® SERIES* furnishes the one special preparation which may assure passing with confidence, instead of failing with insecurity. Examination questions – together with answers – are furnished as the basic vehicle for study so that the mysteries of the examination and its compounding difficulties may be eliminated or diminished by a sure method.

This book is meant to help you pass your examination provided that you qualify and are serious in your objective.

The entire field is reviewed through the huge store of content information which is succinctly presented through a provocative and challenging approach – the question-and-answer method.

A climate of success is established by furnishing the correct answers at the end of each test.

You soon learn to recognize types of questions, forms of questions, and patterns of questioning. You may even begin to anticipate expected outcomes.

You perceive that many questions are repeated or adapted so that you can gain acute insights, which may enable you to score many sure points.

You learn how to confront new questions, or types of questions, and to attack them confidently and work out the correct answers.

You note objectives and emphases, and recognize pitfalls and dangers, so that you may make positive educational adjustments.

Moreover, you are kept fully informed in relation to new concepts, methods, practices, and directions in the field.

You discover that you are actually taking the examination all the time: you are preparing for the examination by "taking" an examination, not by reading extraneous and/or supererogatory textbooks.

In short, this PASSBOOK®, used directedly, should be an important factor in helping you to pass your test.

OCCUPATIONAL COMPETENCY EXAMINATIONS (OCE)

GENERAL

The Occupational Competency Examinations are intended for those individuals experienced in skilled trades or occupations who need to present objective evidence of their competency to become vocational teachers, to obtain academic credit from a higher institution, or to secure teacher certification.

In addition to meeting university admission requirements for fully matriculated students -- and for teacher certification -successful completion of the exam provides opportunity to earn up to 36 semester hours of collegiate credit for applied occupational skills and technical knowledge. The credit may be used toward advanced study and degrees in occupational education in several states.

NATURE OF THE EXAMINATION

The examination consists of two parts -- Written and Performance. The written test covers factual knowledge, technical information, understanding of principles and problem solving abilities related to the occupation. The performance test is designed to sample the manipulative skills required by an occupation. Thus it enables the candidate to demonstrate that he possesses the knowledge and skills that a competent craftsman employs in his daily work.

ADVANTAGES

The Prospective Teacher - Tradesmen and other technically competent persons who wish to enter industrial education training programs.

Industrial Teacher Educators - The OCE Tests provide the industrial teacher educator with an objective and dependable means for assessing the trade competency of applicants for admission to their programs.

Certifying Agencies - The OCE Tests provide an objective method for assessing occupational competence in qualifying for certification.

Directors of Vocational Education Programs - The OCE Tests provide a recruitment and selection procedure that is reliable, objective and fair to all recipients

Candidates for Academic Degrees - The OCE Tests are accepted by many colleges and universities for granting of credit or advanced standing for occupational experience.

PLACE OF EXAMINATION

A network of 36 Area Test Centers has been established throughout the United States in the States listed below. Tests are generally conducted twice a year at these centers, as well as other locations, depending on need.

Alabama	Kentucky	Oregon
Arkansas	Massachusetts	Pennsylvania
California	Michigan	South Dakota
Colorado	Missouri	Tennessee
Connecticut	Montana	Texas
Florida	Nebraska	Utah
Georgia	New Jersey	Vermont
Hawaii	New York	Virginia
Idaho	North Dakota	Washington
Illinois	Ohio	West Virginia
Iowa	Oklahoma	Wisconsin

OCE TESTS OFFERED

Interested candidates are alerted to the occupations listed below as scheduled for examination. Individuals should notify the NOCTI if they wish to be examined in an occupation not listed.

- Air Conditioning and Refrigeration
- Airframe or Power plant Mechanics
- Appliance Repair
- Architectural Drafting
- Auto Body Repair
- Automatic Heating
- Auto Mechanics
- Building Maintenance
- Cabinetmaking and Millwork
- Carpentry
- Commercial and Advertising Art
- Commercial Photography
- Cosmetology
- Data Processing
- Dental Assisting
- Diesel Engine Repair
- Dressmaking
- Electrical Installation
- Electronics Communication
- General Printing Industrial Electronics
- Machine Trades
- Masonry
- Machine Drafting
- Mechanical Technology
- Medical Assisting Offset Lithography
- Ornamental Horticulture
- Plumbing
- Quantity Food Preparation
- Sheet Metal Fabrication
- Small Engine Repair
- Welding

HOW TO REGISTER

For registration information contact Educational Testing Service of Princeton, New Jersey.

HOW TO TAKE A TEST

You have studied long, hard and conscientiously.

With your official admission card in hand, and your heart pounding, you have been admitted to the examination room.

You note that there are several hundred other applicants in the examination room waiting to take the same test.

They all appear to be equally well prepared.

You know that nothing but your best effort will suffice. The "moment of truth" is at hand: you now have to demonstrate objectively, in writing, your knowledge of content and your understanding of subject matter.

You are fighting the most important battle of your life—to pass and/or score high on an examination which will determine your career and provide the economic basis for your livelihood.

What extra, special things should you know and should you do in taking the examination?

I. YOU MUST PASS AN EXAMINATION

A. WHAT EVERY CANDIDATE SHOULD KNOW
Examination applicants often ask us for help in preparing for the written test. What can I study in advance? What kinds of questions will be asked? How will the test be given? How will the papers be graded?

B. HOW ARE EXAMS DEVELOPED?
Examinations are carefully written by trained technicians who are specialists in the field known as "psychological measurement," in consultation with recognized authorities in the field of work that the test will cover. These experts recommend the subject matter areas or skills to be tested; only those knowledges or skills important to your success on the job are included. The most reliable books and source materials available are used as references. Together, the experts and technicians judge the difficulty level of the questions.
Test technicians know how to phrase questions so that the problem is clearly stated. Their ethics do not permit "trick" or "catch" questions. Questions may have been tried out on sample groups, or subjected to statistical analysis, to determine their usefulness.
Written tests are often used in combination with performance tests, ratings of training and experience, and oral interviews. All of these measures combine to form the best-known means of finding the right person for the right job.

II. HOW TO PASS THE WRITTEN TEST

A. BASIC STEPS

1) Study the announcement

How, then, can you know what subjects to study? Our best answer is: "Learn as much as possible about the class of positions for which you've applied." The exam will test the knowledge, skills and abilities needed to do the work.

Your most valuable source of information about the position you want is the official exam announcement. This announcement lists the training and experience qualifications. Check these standards and apply only if you come reasonably close to meeting them. Many jurisdictions preview the written test in the exam announcement by including a section called "Knowledge and Abilities Required," "Scope of the Examination," or some similar heading. Here you will find out specifically what fields will be tested.

2) Choose appropriate study materials

If the position for which you are applying is technical or advanced, you will read more advanced, specialized material. If you are already familiar with the basic principles of your field, elementary textbooks would waste your time. Concentrate on advanced textbooks and technical periodicals. Think through the concepts and review difficult problems in your field.

These are all general sources. You can get more ideas on your own initiative, following these leads. For example, training manuals and publications of the government agency which employs workers in your field can be useful, particularly for technical and professional positions. A letter or visit to the government department involved may result in more specific study suggestions, and certainly will provide you with a more definite idea of the exact nature of the position you are seeking.

3) Study this book!

III. KINDS OF TESTS

Tests are used for purposes other than measuring knowledge and ability to perform specified duties. For some positions, it is equally important to test ability to make adjustments to new situations or to profit from training. In others, basic mental abilities not dependent on information are essential. Questions which test these things may not appear as pertinent to the duties of the position as those which test for knowledge and information. Yet they are often highly important parts of a fair examination. For very general questions, it is almost impossible to help you direct your study efforts. What we can do is to point out some of the more common of these general abilities needed in public service positions and describe some typical questions.

1) General information

Broad, general information has been found useful for predicting job success in some kinds of work. This is tested in a variety of ways, from vocabulary lists to questions about current events. Basic background in some field of work, such as sociology or economics, may be sampled in a group of questions. Often these are principles which have become familiar to most persons through exposure rather than through formal training. It is difficult to advise you how to study for these questions; being alert to the world around you is our best suggestion.

2) Verbal ability

An example of an ability needed in many positions is verbal or language ability. Verbal ability is, in brief, the ability to use and understand words. Vocabulary and grammar tests are typical measures of this ability. Reading comprehension or paragraph interpretation questions are common in many kinds of civil service tests. You are given a paragraph of written material and asked to find its central meaning.

IV. KINDS OF QUESTIONS

1. Multiple-choice Questions

Most popular of the short-answer questions is the "multiple choice" or "best answer" question. It can be used, for example, to test for factual knowledge, ability to solve problems or judgment in meeting situations found at work.

A multiple-choice question is normally one of three types:
- It can begin with an incomplete statement followed by several possible endings. You are to find the one ending which best completes the statement, although some of the others may not be entirely wrong.
- It can also be a complete statement in the form of a question which is answered by choosing one of the statements listed.
- It can be in the form of a problem – again you select the best answer.

Here is an example of a multiple-choice question with a discussion which should give you some clues as to the method for choosing the right answer:

When an employee has a complaint about his assignment, the action which will best help him overcome his difficulty is to
  A. discuss his difficulty with his coworkers
  B. take the problem to the head of the organization
  C. take the problem to the person who gave him the assignment
  D. say nothing to anyone about his complaint

In answering this question, you should study each of the choices to find which is best. Consider choice "A" – Certainly an employee may discuss his complaint with fellow employees, but no change or improvement can result, and the complaint remains unresolved. Choice "B" is a poor choice since the head of the organization probably does not know what assignment you have been given, and taking your problem to him is known as "going over the head" of the supervisor. The supervisor, or person who made the assignment, is the person who can clarify it or correct any injustice. Choice "C" is, therefore, correct. To say nothing, as in choice "D," is unwise. Supervisors have and interest in knowing the problems employees are facing, and the employee is seeking a solution to his problem.

2. True/False

3. Matching Questions

Matching an answer from a column of choices within another column.

V. RECORDING YOUR ANSWERS

Computer terminals are used more and more today for many different kinds of exams.

For an examination with very few applicants, you may be told to record your answers in the test booklet itself. Separate answer sheets are much more common. If this separate answer sheet is to be scored by machine – and this is often the case – it is highly important that you mark your answers correctly in order to get credit.

VI. BEFORE THE TEST

YOUR PHYSICAL CONDITION IS IMPORTANT

If you are not well, you can't do your best work on tests. If you are half asleep, you can't do your best either. Here are some tips:

1) Get about the same amount of sleep you usually get. Don't stay up all night before the test, either partying or worrying—DON'T DO IT!
2) If you wear glasses, be sure to wear them when you go to take the test. This goes for hearing aids, too.
3) If you have any physical problems that may keep you from doing your best, be sure to tell the person giving the test. If you are sick or in poor health, you relay cannot do your best on any test. You can always come back and take the test some other time.

Common sense will help you find procedures to follow to get ready for an examination. Too many of us, however, overlook these sensible measures. Indeed, nervousness and fatigue have been found to be the most serious reasons why applicants fail to do their best on civil service tests. Here is a list of reminders:

- Begin your preparation early – Don't wait until the last minute to go scurrying around for books and materials or to find out what the position is all about.
- Prepare continuously – An hour a night for a week is better than an all-night cram session. This has been definitely established. What is more, a night a week for a month will return better dividends than crowding your study into a shorter period of time.
- Locate the place of the exam – You have been sent a notice telling you when and where to report for the examination. If the location is in a different town or otherwise unfamiliar to you, it would be well to inquire the best route and learn something about the building.
- Relax the night before the test – Allow your mind to rest. Do not study at all that night. Plan some mild recreation or diversion; then go to bed early and get a good night's sleep.
- Get up early enough to make a leisurely trip to the place for the test – This way unforeseen events, traffic snarls, unfamiliar buildings, etc. will not upset you.
- Dress comfortably – A written test is not a fashion show. You will be known by number and not by name, so wear something comfortable.
- Leave excess paraphernalia at home – Shopping bags and odd bundles will get in your way. You need bring only the items mentioned in the official notice you received; usually everything you need is provided. Do not bring reference books to the exam. They will only confuse those last minutes and be taken away from you when in the test room.

- Arrive somewhat ahead of time – If because of transportation schedules you must get there very early, bring a newspaper or magazine to take your mind off yourself while waiting.
- Locate the examination room – When you have found the proper room, you will be directed to the seat or part of the room where you will sit. Sometimes you are given a sheet of instructions to read while you are waiting. Do not fill out any forms until you are told to do so; just read them and be prepared.
- Relax and prepare to listen to the instructions
- If you have any physical problem that may keep you from doing your best, be sure to tell the test administrator. If you are sick or in poor health, you really cannot do your best on the exam. You can come back and take the test some other time.

VII. AT THE TEST

The day of the test is here and you have the test booklet in your hand. The temptation to get going is very strong. Caution! There is more to success than knowing the right answers. You must know how to identify your papers and understand variations in the type of short-answer question used in this particular examination. Follow these suggestions for maximum results from your efforts:

1) Cooperate with the monitor

The test administrator has a duty to create a situation in which you can be as much at ease as possible. He will give instructions, tell you when to begin, check to see that you are marking your answer sheet correctly, and so on. He is not there to guard you, although he will see that your competitors do not take unfair advantage. He wants to help you do your best.

2) Listen to all instructions

Don't jump the gun! Wait until you understand all directions. In most civil service tests you get more time than you need to answer the questions. So don't be in a hurry. Read each word of instructions until you clearly understand the meaning. Study the examples, listen to all announcements and follow directions. Ask questions if you do not understand what to do.

3) Identify your papers

Civil service exams are usually identified by number only. You will be assigned a number; you must not put your name on your test papers. Be sure to copy your number correctly. Since more than one exam may be given, copy your exact examination title.

4) Plan your time

Unless you are told that a test is a "speed" or "rate of work" test, speed itself is usually not important. Time enough to answer all the questions will be provided, but this does not mean that you have all day. An overall time limit has been set. Divide the total time (in minutes) by the number of questions to determine the approximate time you have for each question.

5) Do not linger over difficult questions

If you come across a difficult question, mark it with a paper clip (useful to have along) and come back to it when you have been through the booklet. One caution if you do this – be sure to skip a number on your answer sheet as well. Check often to be sure that you have not lost your place and that you are marking in the row numbered the same as the question you are answering.

6) Read the questions

Be sure you know what the question asks! Many capable people are unsuccessful because they failed to read the questions correctly.

7) Answer all questions

Unless you have been instructed that a penalty will be deducted for incorrect answers, it is better to guess than to omit a question.

8) Speed tests

It is often better NOT to guess on speed tests. It has been found that on timed tests people are tempted to spend the last few seconds before time is called in marking answers at random – without even reading them – in the hope of picking up a few extra points. To discourage this practice, the instructions may warn you that your score will be "corrected" for guessing. That is, a penalty will be applied. The incorrect answers will be deducted from the correct ones, or some other penalty formula will be used.

9) Review your answers

If you finish before time is called, go back to the questions you guessed or omitted to give them further thought. Review other answers if you have time.

10) Return your test materials

If you are ready to leave before others have finished or time is called, take ALL your materials to the monitor and leave quietly. Never take any test material with you. The monitor can discover whose papers are not complete, and taking a test booklet may be grounds for disqualification.

VIII. EXAMINATION TECHNIQUES

1) Read the general instructions carefully. These are usually printed on the first page of the exam booklet. As a rule, these instructions refer to the timing of the examination; the fact that you should not start work until the signal and must stop work at a signal, etc. If there are any special instructions, such as a choice of questions to be answered, make sure that you note this instruction carefully.

2) When you are ready to start work on the examination, that is as soon as the signal has been given, read the instructions to each question booklet, underline any key words or phrases, such as least, best, outline, describe and the like. In this way you will tend to answer as requested rather than discover on reviewing your paper that you listed without describing, that you selected the worst choice rather than the best choice, etc.

3) If the examination is of the objective or multiple-choice type – that is, each question will also give a series of possible answers: A, B, C or D, and you are called upon to select the best answer and write the letter next to that answer on your answer paper – it is advisable to start answering each question in turn. There may be anywhere from 50 to 100 such questions in the three or four hours allotted and you can see how much time would be taken if you read through all the questions before beginning to answer any. Furthermore, if you

come across a question or group of questions which you know would be difficult to answer, it would undoubtedly affect your handling of all the other questions.

4) If the examination is of the essay type and contains but a few questions, it is a moot point as to whether you should read all the questions before starting to answer any one. Of course, if you are given a choice – say five out of seven and the like – then it is essential to read all the questions so you can eliminate the two that are most difficult. If, however, you are asked to answer all the questions, there may be danger in trying to answer the easiest one first because you may find that you will spend too much time on it. The best technique is to answer the first question, then proceed to the second, etc.

5) Time your answers. Before the exam begins, write down the time it started, then add the time allowed for the examination and write down the time it must be completed, then divide the time available somewhat as follows:
   - If 3-1/2 hours are allowed, that would be 210 minutes. If you have 80 objective-type questions, that would be an average of 2-1/2 minutes per question. Allow yourself no more than 2 minutes per question, or a total of 160 minutes, which will permit about 50 minutes to review.
   - If for the time allotment of 210 minutes there are 7 essay questions to answer, that would average about 30 minutes a question. Give yourself only 25 minutes per question so that you have about 35 minutes to review.

6) The most important instruction is to read each question and make sure you know what is wanted. The second most important instruction is to time yourself properly so that you answer every question. The third most important instruction is to answer every question. Guess if you have to but include something for each question. Remember that you will receive no credit for a blank and will probably receive some credit if you write something in answer to an essay question. If you guess a letter – say "B" for a multiple-choice question – you may have guessed right. If you leave a blank as an answer to a multiple-choice question, the examiners may respect your feelings but it will not add a point to your score. Some exams may penalize you for wrong answers, so in such cases only, you may not want to guess unless you have some basis for your answer.

7) Suggestions
   a. Objective-type questions
      1. Examine the question booklet for proper sequence of pages and questions
      2. Read all instructions carefully
      3. Skip any question which seems too difficult; return to it after all other questions have been answered
      4. Apportion your time properly; do not spend too much time on any single question or group of questions
      5. Note and underline key words – all, most, fewest, least, best, worst, same, opposite, etc.
      6. Pay particular attention to negatives
      7. Note unusual option, e.g., unduly long, short, complex, different or similar in content to the body of the question
      8. Observe the use of "hedging" words – probably, may, most likely, etc.

9. Make sure that your answer is put next to the same number as the question
10. Do not second-guess unless you have good reason to believe the second answer is definitely more correct
11. Cross out original answer if you decide another answer is more accurate; do not erase until you are ready to hand your paper in
12. Answer all questions; guess unless instructed otherwise
13. Leave time for review

b. Essay questions
1. Read each question carefully
2. Determine exactly what is wanted. Underline key words or phrases.
3. Decide on outline or paragraph answer
4. Include many different points and elements unless asked to develop any one or two points or elements
5. Show impartiality by giving pros and cons unless directed to select one side only
6. Make and write down any assumptions you find necessary to answer the questions
7. Watch your English, grammar, punctuation and choice of words
8. Time your answers; don't crowd material

8) Answering the essay question

Most essay questions can be answered by framing the specific response around several key words or ideas. Here are a few such key words or ideas:

M's: manpower, materials, methods, money, management
P's: purpose, program, policy, plan, procedure, practice, problems, pitfalls, personnel, public relations

a. Six basic steps in handling problems:
1. Preliminary plan and background development
2. Collect information, data and facts
3. Analyze and interpret information, data and facts
4. Analyze and develop solutions as well as make recommendations
5. Prepare report and sell recommendations
6. Install recommendations and follow up effectiveness

b. Pitfalls to avoid
1. Taking things for granted – A statement of the situation does not necessarily imply that each of the elements is necessarily true; for example, a complaint may be invalid and biased so that all that can be taken for granted is that a complaint has been registered
2. Considering only one side of a situation – Wherever possible, indicate several alternatives and then point out the reasons you selected the best one
3. Failing to indicate follow up – Whenever your answer indicates action on your part, make certain that you will take proper follow-up action to see how successful your recommendations, procedures or actions turn out to be
4. Taking too long in answering any single question – Remember to time your answers properly

EXAMINATION SECTION

EXAMINATION SECTION
TEST 1

DIRECTIONS: Each question or incomplete statement is followed by several suggested answers or completions. Select the one that BEST answers the question or completes the statement. *PRINT THE LETTER OF THE CORRECT ANSWER IN THE SPACE AT THE RIGHT.*

1. Linseed oil putty would MOST likely be used to secure glass in _____ windows.

    A. steel casement B. aluminum jalousie
    C. wood double hung D. aluminum storm

2. Of the following, the one type of glass that should NOT be cut with the ordinary type glass cutter is _____ glass.

    A. safety B. plate C. wire D. herculite

3. Thermopane is made of two sheets of glass separated by

    A. a sheet of celluloid B. wire mesh
    C. an air space D. mica

4. Glass is NEVER cut so that it fits snugly inside the frame of a steel casement window. Of the following, the MAIN reason for allowing this space between the glass and the side of the frame is to

    A. prevent cracking of the glass in cold weather
    B. permit the glass to be lined up properly
    C. allow space for the putty
    D. eliminate the necessity of polishing the edges of the glass

5. Glass is held in steel sash by means of

    A. points B. clips C. plates D. blocks

6. When nailing felt to a roof, the nails should be driven through a

    A. tinned disc B. steel washer
    C. brass plate D. plastic bushing

7. An opening in a parapet wall for draining water from a roof is MOST often called a

    A. leader B. gutter C. downspout D. scupper

8. Roofing nails are usually

    A. brass B. cement coated
    C. galvanized D. nickel plated

9. A *street ell* is a fitting having

    A. male threads at both ends
    B. male threads at one end and female threads at the other end
    C. female threads at both ends
    D. male threads at one end and a solder connection at the other end

10. Of the following pieces of equipment, the one on which you would MOST likely find a safety (pop-off) valve is a(n)

    A. hot air furnace
    B. air conditioning compressor
    C. hot water heater
    D. dehumidifier

11. Compression fittings are MOST often used with

    A. cast iron bell and spigot pipe
    B. steel flange pipe
    C. copper tubing
    D. transite

12. Water hammer is BEST eliminated by

    A. increasing the size of all the piping
    B. installing an air chamber
    C. replacing the valve seats with neoprene gaskets
    D. flushing the system to remove corrosion

13. The BEST type of pipe to use in a gas line in a domestic installation is

    A. black iron   B. galvanized iron
    C. cast iron   D. wrought steel

14. If there is a pinhole in the float of a toilet tank, the

    A. water will flush continually
    B. toilet cannot flush
    C. tank cannot be filled with water
    D. valve will not shut off so water will overflow into the overflow tube

15. Condensation of moisture in humid weather occurs MOST often on _____ pipe(s).

    A. sewage   B. gas
    C. hot water   D. cold water

16. A gas appliance should be connected to a gas line by means of a(n)

    A. union   B. right and left coupling
    C. elbow   D. close nipple

17. A PRINCIPAL difference between a pipe thread and a machine thread is that the pipe thread is

    A. tapered   B. finer   C. flat   D. longer

18. When joining galvanized iron pipe, pipe joint compound is placed on

    A. the female threads only
    B. the male threads only
    C. both the male and female threads
    D. either the male or the female threads depending on the type of fitting

19. If moisture is trapped between the layers of a 3-ply roof, the heat of a summer day will

    A. dry the roof out
    B. cause blisters to be formed in the roofing
    C. rot the felt material
    D. have no effect on the roofing

20. Of the following, the metal MOST often used for leaders and gutters is

    A. monel
    B. brass
    C. steel
    D. galvanized iron

21. When drilling a small hole in sheet copper, the BEST practice is to

    A. make a dent with a center punch first
    B. put some cutting oil at the point you intend to drill
    C. use a slow speed drill to prevent overheating
    D. use an auger type bit

22. The reason for annealing sheet copper is to make it

    A. soft and easier to work
    B. more resistant to weather
    C. easier to solder
    D. harder and more resistant to blows

23. In draw filing,

    A. only the edge of the file is used
    B. a triangle file is generally used
    C. the file is pulled toward the mechanic's body in filing
    D. the file must have a safe edge

24. The type of paint that uses water as a thinner is

    A. enamel   B. latex   C. shellac   D. lacquer

25. The reason for placing a 6" sub-base of cinders under a concrete sidewalk is to

    A. provide flexibility in the surface
    B. permit drainage of water
    C. prevent chemicals in the soil from damaging the sidewalk
    D. allow room for the concrete to expand

26. The BEST material to use to lubricate a door lock is

    A. penetrating oil
    B. pike oil
    C. graphite
    D. light grease

27. Assume that the color of the flame from a gas stove is bright yellow. To correct this, you should

    A. close the air flap
    B. open the air flap
    C. increase the gas pressure
    D. increase the size of the gas opening

28. In a 110-220 volt three-wire circuit, the neutral wire is usually

   A. black B. red C. white D. green

29. Brushes on fractional horsepower universal motors are MOST often made of

   A. flexible copper strands B. rigid carbon blocks
   C. thin wire strips D. collector rings

30. Leaks from the stem of a faucet can generally be stopped by replacing the

   A. bibb washer B. seat C. packing D. gasket

31. Of the following, the BEST procedure to follow with a frozen water pipe is to

   A. allow the pipe to thaw out by itself as the weather gets warmer
   B. put anti-freeze into the pipe above the section that is frozen
   C. turn on the hot water heater
   D. open the faucet closest to the frozen pipe and warm the pipe with a blow torch, starting at this point

32. The one of the following that is NOT usually changed by a central air conditioning system is the

   A. volume of air in the system B. humidity of the air
   C. dust in the air D. air pressure of the system

33. The temperature of a domestic hot water system is MOST often controlled by a(n)

   A. relief valve B. aquastat C. barometer D. thermostat

34. Draft in a chimney is MOST often controlled by a(n)

   A. damper B. gate
   C. orifice D. cross connection

35. Assume that a refrigerator motor operates continuously for excessively long periods of time.
    The FIRST item you should check to locate the defect is the

   A. plug in the outlet
   B. door gasket
   C. direction of rotation of the motor
   D. motor switch

36. Assume that after replacing a defective motor for a large electric fan, you find that the fan is rotating in the wrong direction.
    If the motor is a split phase motor, with the shaft at one end only, the trouble could be CORRECTED by

   A. reversing the fan on its shaft
   B. turning the motor end for end
   C. interchanging the connections on the field terminals of the motor
   D. reversing the plug in the electric outlet

37. In order to properly hang a door, shims are frequently inserted under the hinges. These shims are MOST often made of

    A. cardboard
    B. sheet steel
    C. bakelite
    D. the same materials as the hinges

37.____

38. Flooring nails are usually _____ nails.

    A. casing   B. common   C. cut   D. clinch

38.____

39. Over a doorway, to support brick, you will usually find

    A. steel angles   B. hanger bolts
    C. wooden headers   D. stirrups

39.____

40. Insulation of steam pipes is MOST often done with

    A. asbestos   B. celotex   C. alundum   D. sheathing

40.____

41. Assume that only the first few coils of a hot water convector used for heating a room are hot.
    To correct this, you should FIRST

    A. increase the water pressure
    B. increase the water temperature
    C. bleed the air out of the convector
    D. clean the convector pipes

41.____

42. The MAIN reason for grounding the outer sheel of an electric fixture is to

    A. provide additional support for the fixture
    B. reduce the cost of installation of the fixture
    C. provide a terminal to which the wires can be attached
    D. reduce the chance of electric shock

42.____

43. In woodwork, countersinking is MOST often done for

    A. lag screws   B. carriage bolts
    C. hanger bolts   D. flat head screws

43.____

44. Bridging is MOST often used in connection with

    A. door frames   B. window openings
    C. floor joists   D. stud walls

44.____

45. A saddle is part of a

    A. doorway   B. window
    C. stair well   D. bulkhead

45.____

46. To make it easier to drive screws into hard wood, it is BEST to

   A. use a screwdriver that is longer than that used for soft wood
   B. rub the threads of the screw on a bar of soap
   C. oil the screw threads
   D. use a square shank screwdriver assisted by a wrench

47. In using a doweled joint to make a repair of a wooden door, it is important to remember that the dowel

   A. hole must be smaller in diameter than the dowel so that there is a tight fit
   B. hole must be longer than the dowel to provide a room for excess glue
   C. must be of the same type of wood as the door frame
   D. must be held in place by a small screw while waiting for the glue to set

48. The edges of MOST finished wood flooring are

   A. tongue and groove
   B. mortise and tenon
   C. bevel and miter
   D. lap and scarf

49. For the SMOOTHEST finish, sanding of wood should be done

   A. in a circular direction
   B. diagonally against the grain
   C. across the grain
   D. parallel with the grain

50. To prevent splintering of wood when boring a hole through it, the BEST practice is to

   A. drill at a slow speed
   B. use a scrap piece to back up the work
   C. use an auger bit
   D. ease up the pressure on the drill when the drill is almost through the wood

---

KEY (CORRECT ANSWERS)

1. C	11. C	21. A	31. D	41. C
2. D	12. B	22. A	32. D	42. D
3. C	13. A	23. C	33. B	43. D
4. A	14. D	24. B	34. A	44. C
5. B	15. D	25. B	35. B	45. A
6. A	16. B	26. C	36. C	46. B
7. D	17. A	27. B	37. A	47. B
8. C	18. B	28. C	38. C	48. A
9. B	19. B	29. B	39. A	49. D
10. C	20. D	30. C	40. A	50. B

TEST 2

DIRECTIONS: Each question or incomplete statement is followed by several suggested answers or completions. Select the one that BEST answers the question or completes the statement. *PRINT THE LETTER OF THE CORRECT ANSWER IN THE SPACE AT THE RIGHT.*

1. A *speed nut* has
   A. no threads
   B. threads that are coarser than a standard nut
   C. threads that are finer than s standard nut
   D. fewer threads than a standard nut

2. The BEST tool to use to remove the burr and sharp edge resulting from cutting tubing with a tube cutter is a
   A. file   B. scraper   C. reamer   D. knife

3. A router is used PRINCIPALLY to
   A. clean pipe
   B. cut grooves in wood
   C. bend electric conduit
   D. sharpen tools

4. The principle of operation of a sabre saw is MOST similar to that of a _____ saw.
   A. circular   B. radial   C. swing   D. jig

5. A full thread cutting set would have both taps and
   A. cutters   B. bushings   C. dies   D. plugs

6. The proper flux to use for soldering electric wire connections is
   A. rosin
   B. killed acid
   C. borax
   D. zinc chloride

7. A fusestat differs from an ordinary plug fuse in that a fusestat has
   A. less current carrying capacity
   B. different size threads
   C. an aluminum shell instead of a copper shell
   D. no threads

8. A grounding type 120-volt receptacle differs from an ordinary electric receptacle MAINLY in that a grounding receptacle
   A. is larger than the ordinary receptacle
   B. has openings for a three prong plug
   C. can be used for larger machinery
   D. has a built-in circuit breaker

9. A carbide tip is MOST often found on a bit used for drilling
   A. concrete   B. wood   C. steel   D. brass

10. The MAIN reason for using oil on an oilstone is to   10.___

    A. make the surface of the stone smoother
    B. prevent clogging of the pores of the stone
    C. reduce the number of times the stone has to be *dressed*
    D. prevent gouging of the stone's surface

11. The sum of the following numbers, 1 3/4, 3 1/6, 5 1/2, 6 5/8, and 9 1/4, is   11.___

    A. 26 1/8   B. 26 1/4   C. 26 1/2   D. 26 3/4

12. If a piece of plywood measures 5' 1 1/4" x 3' 2 1/2", the number of square feet in this   12.___
    board is MOST NEARLY

    A. 15.8   B. 16.1   C. 16.4   D. 16.7

13. Assume that in quantity purchases the city receives a discount of 33 1/3%.   13.___
    If a one gallon can of paint retails at $5.33 per gallon, the cost of 375 gallons of this
    paint is MOST NEARLY

    A. $1,332.50   B. $1,332.75   C. $1,333.00   D. $1,333.25

14. Assume that eight barrels of cement together weigh a total of 3004 lbs. and 12 oz.   14.___
    If there are four bags of cement per barrel, then the weight of one bag of cement is
    MOST NEARLY _____ lbs.

    A. 93.1   B. 93.5   C. 93.9   D. 94.3

15. Assume that one man cuts 50 nameplates per hour, whereas his co-worker cuts 55   15.___
    nameplates per hour.
    At the end of 7 hours, the first man will have cut fewer nameplates than the second
    man by

    A. 9.3%   B. 9.5%   C. 9.7%   D. 9.9%

16. Under the same conditions, the one of the following that dries the FASTEST is   16.___

    A. shellac   B. varnish   C. enamel   D. lacquer

17. Interior wood trim in a building is MOST often made of   17.___

    A. hemlock   B. pine   C. cedar   D. oak

18. Gaskets are seldom made of   18.___

    A. rubber   B. lead   C. asbestos   D. vinyl

19. Toggle bolts are MOST frequently used to   19.___

    A. fasten shelf supports to a hollow block wall
    B. fasten furniture legs to table tops
    C. anchor machinery to a concrete floor
    D. join two pieces of sheet metal

20. Rubber will deteriorate FASTEST when it is constantly in contact with   20.___

    A. air   B. water   C. oil   D. soapsuds

21. Stoppage of water flow is often caused by dirt <u>accumulating</u> in an elbow.
    As used in the above sentence, the word <u>accumulating</u> means MOST NEARLY

    A. clogging   B. collecting   C. rusting   D. confined

22. The surface of the metal was <u>embossed</u>.
    As used in the above sentence, the word <u>embossed</u> means MOST NEARLY

    A. polished   B. rough   C. raised   D. painted

Questions 23-24.

DIRECTIONS: Questions 23 and 24 are to be answered in accordance with the following paragraph.

When fixing an upper sash cord, you must also remove the lower sash. To do this, the parting strip between the sash must be removed. Now remove the cover from the weight box channel, cut off the cord as before, and pull it over the pulleys. Pull your new cord over the pulleys and down into the channel, where it may be fastened to the weight. The cord for an upper sash is cut off 1" or 2" below the pulley with the weight resting on the floor of the pocket and the cord held taut. These measurements allow for slight stretching of the cord. When the cord is cut to length, it can be pulled up over the pulley and tied with a single common knot in the end to fit into the socket in the sash groove. If the knot protrudes beyond the face of the sash, tap it gently to flatten. In this way, it will not become frayed from constant rubbing against the groove.

23. When repairing the upper sash cord, the FIRST thing to do is to

    A. remove the lower sash
    B. cut the existing sash cord
    C. remove the parting strip
    D. measure the length of new cord necessary

24. According to the above paragraph, the rope may become frayed if the

    A. pulley is too small   B. knot sticks out
    C. cord is too long   D. weight is too heavy

25. In the repair of the sash cord mentioned in the paragraph for Questions 23 and 24, the MAIN reason for cutting off the sash cord below the bottom of the pulley is to

    A. prevent the cord from tangling
    B. save on amount of cord used
    C. prevent the sash weight from hitting the bottom of the frame in use
    D. provide room for tying the knot

26. Of the following drawings, the one that would be considered an *elevation* of a building is the

    A. floor plan   B. front view   C. cross section   D. site plan

27. On a plan, the symbol shown at the right USUALLY represents a(n)

    A. duplex receptacle   B. electric switch
    C. ceiling outlet   D. pull box

28. On a plan, the symbol _____ - _____ - USUALLY represents a
    A. center line
    B. hidden outline
    C. long break
    D. dimension line

29. Assume that on a plan you see the following: 1/4" - 20 NC-2. This refers to the
    A. diameter of a hole
    B. size and type of screw thread
    C. taper of a pin
    D. scale at which the plan is drawn

30. In reference to the above sketch, the length of the diagonal part of the plate indicated by the question mark is MOST NEARLY
    A. 13"   B. 14"   C. 15"   D. 16"

31. To increase the workability of concrete without changing its strength, the BEST procedure to follow is to increase the percentage of
    A. water
    B. cement and sand
    C. cement and water
    D. water and sand

32. The MAIN reason for covering freshly poured concrete with tar paper is to
    A. prevent evaporation of water
    B. stop people from walking on the concrete
    C. protect the concrete from rain
    D. keep back any earth that may fall on the concrete

33. The MAIN reason for using air-entrained cement in sidewalks is to
    A. protect the concrete from the effects of freezing
    B. color the concrete
    C. speed up the setting time of the concrete
    D. make the concrete more workable

34. Assume that a reinforcing bar used for concrete is badly rusted. Before using this bar,

    A. it is not necessary to remove any rust
    B. only loose rust need be removed
    C. all rust should be removed
    D. all rust should be removed and a coat of red lead paint is applied

35. Assume that freshly poured concrete has been exposed to freezing temperatures for 6 hours.
    In all likelihood, this concrete

    A. has been permanently damaged
    B. will harden properly as soon as the air temperature warms up
    C. will harden properly even though the temperature remains below freezing
    D. will eventually harden properly, but it will take much longer than usual

36. Assume that concrete for a floor in a play yard is to be placed directly on the earth. On checking, you find that, because of a recent rain, the earth is damp.
    You should

    A. wait till the sun dries the earth before placing the concrete
    B. use a waterproofing material between the concrete slab and the earth
    C. use less water in the concrete mix
    D. ignore the damp earth and place the concrete as you normally would

37. The MAJOR disadvantage of *floating* the surface of concrete too much is that the

    A. surface will become too rough
    B. surface will become weak and will wear rapidly
    C. initial set will be disturbed
    D. concrete cannot be cured properly

38. In addition to water and sand, mortar mix for a cinder block wall is usually made of

    A. gravel and lime
    B. plaster and cement
    C. gravel and cement
    D. lime and cement

39. The *nominal* size of a standard cinder block is

    A. 8" x 6" x 16"
    B. 8" x 8" x 16"
    C. 8" x 12" x 12"
    D. 6" x 8" x 12"

40. The *bond* of a brick wall refers to the

    A. arrangement of headers and stretchers
    B. time it takes for the mortar to set
    C. way a brick wall is tied in to an intersecting wall
    D. type of mortar used in the wall

41. The purpose of *tooling* when erecting a brick wall is to

    A. cut the brick to fit into a small space
    B. insure that the brick is laid level
    C. compact the mortar at the joints
    D. hold the brick in place till the mortar sets

42. Mortar is BEST cleaned off the face of a brick wall by using 42.___

    A. muriatic acid B. lye
    C. oxalic acid D. sodium hypochlorite

43. A brick wall is *pointed* to 43.___

    A. make sure it is the correct height
    B. repair the mortar joints
    C. set the brick in place
    D. arrange the mortar bed before setting the brick

44. The second coat in a three-coat plaster job is the _____ coat. 44.___

    A. scratch B. brown C. putty D. lime

45. To repair fine cracks in a plastered wall, the PROPER material to use is 45.___

    A. lime B. cement wash
    C. perlite D. spackle

46. Gypsum lath for plastering is purchased in 46.___

    A. strips 5/16" x 1 1/2" x 4'
    B. rolls 3/8" x 48" x 96"
    C. boards 1/2" x 16" x 48"
    D. sheets 5/16" x 27" x 96"

47. The PRINCIPAL reason for using acoustic tile instead of ordinary tile is that the acoustic tile 47.___

    A. deadens sound B. is easier to apply
    C. is longer lasting D. costs less

48. The MAXIMUM thickness of the finish coat of white plaster is MOST NEARLY 48.___

    A. 1/8" B. 1/4" C. 3/8" D. 1/2"

49. When using tape to conceal joints in dry wall construction, the FIRST operation is 49.___

    A. channelling the grooves between boards
    B. applying cement to the joints
    C. sanding the edges of the joints
    D. packing the tape into the joints

50. For the FIRST coat of plaster on wire lath, plaster of paris is mixed with 50.___

    A. cement B. sand C. lime D. mortar

KEY (CORRECT ANSWERS)

1. A	11. B	21. B	31. C	41. C
2. C	12. C	22. C	32. A	42. A
3. B	13. A	23. C	33. A	43. B
4. D	14. C	24. B	34. B	44. B
5. C	15. D	25. C	35. A	45. D
6. A	16. D	26. B	36. D	46. C
7. B	17. B	27. C	37. B	47. A
8. B	18. D	28. A	38. D	48. A
9. A	19. A	29. B	39. B	49. B
10. B	20. C	30. A	40. A	50. B

EXAMINATION SECTION
TEST 1

DIRECTIONS: Each question or incomplete statement is followed by several suggested answers or completions. Select the one that BEST answers the question or completes the statement. *PRINT THE LETTER OF THE CORRECT ANSWER IN THE SPACE AT THE RIGHT.*

1.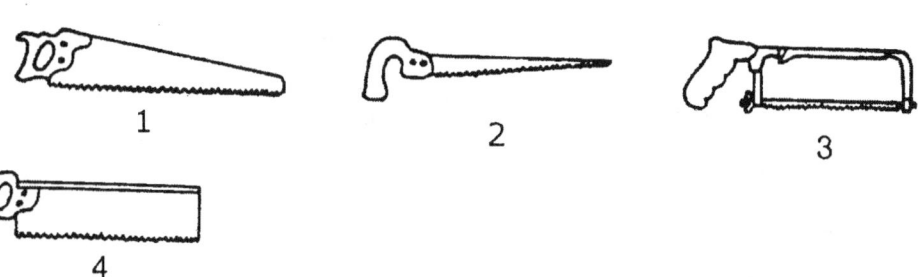
   The saw that is used PRINCIPALLY where curved cuts are to be made is numbered
   A. 1 B. 2 C. 3 D. 4

   1.____

2.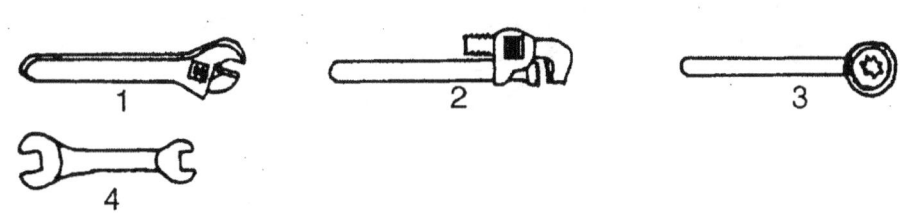
   The wrench that is used PRINCIPALLY for pipe work is numbered
   A. 1 B. 2 C. 3 D. 4

   2.____

3.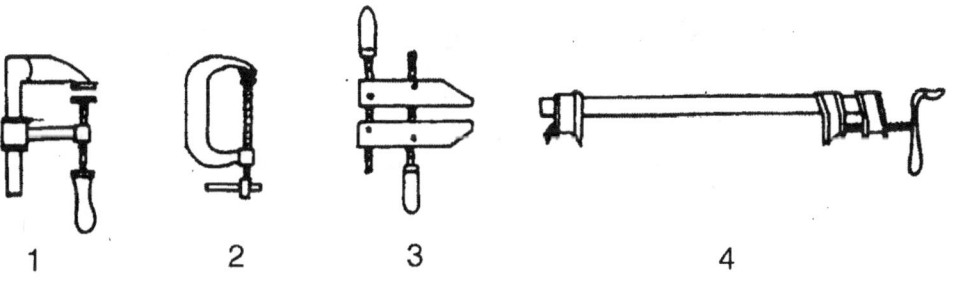
   The carpenter's *hand screw* is numbered
   A. 1 B. 2 C. 3 D. 4

   3.____

4.

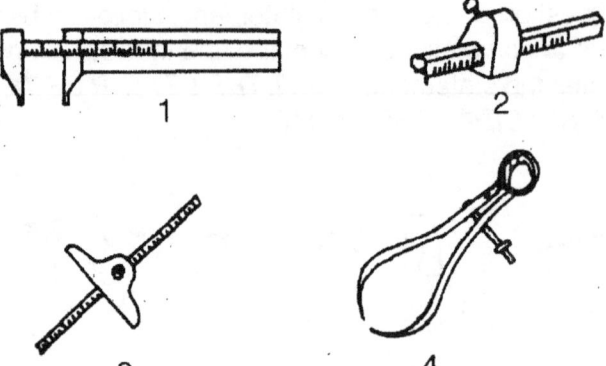

The tool used to measure the depth of a hole is numbered

A. 1   B. 2   C. 3   D. 4

5.

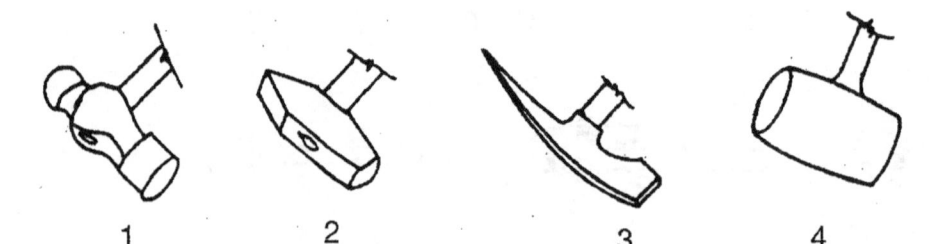

The tool that is BEST suited for use with a wood chisel is numbered

A. 1   B. 2   C. 3   D. 4

6.

The screw head that would be tightened with an *Allen* wrench is numbered

A. 1   B. 2   C. 3   D. 4

7.

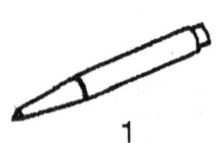 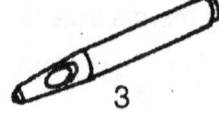

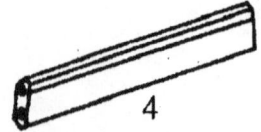

The center punch is numbered

A. 1   B. 2   C. 3   D. 4

3 (#1)

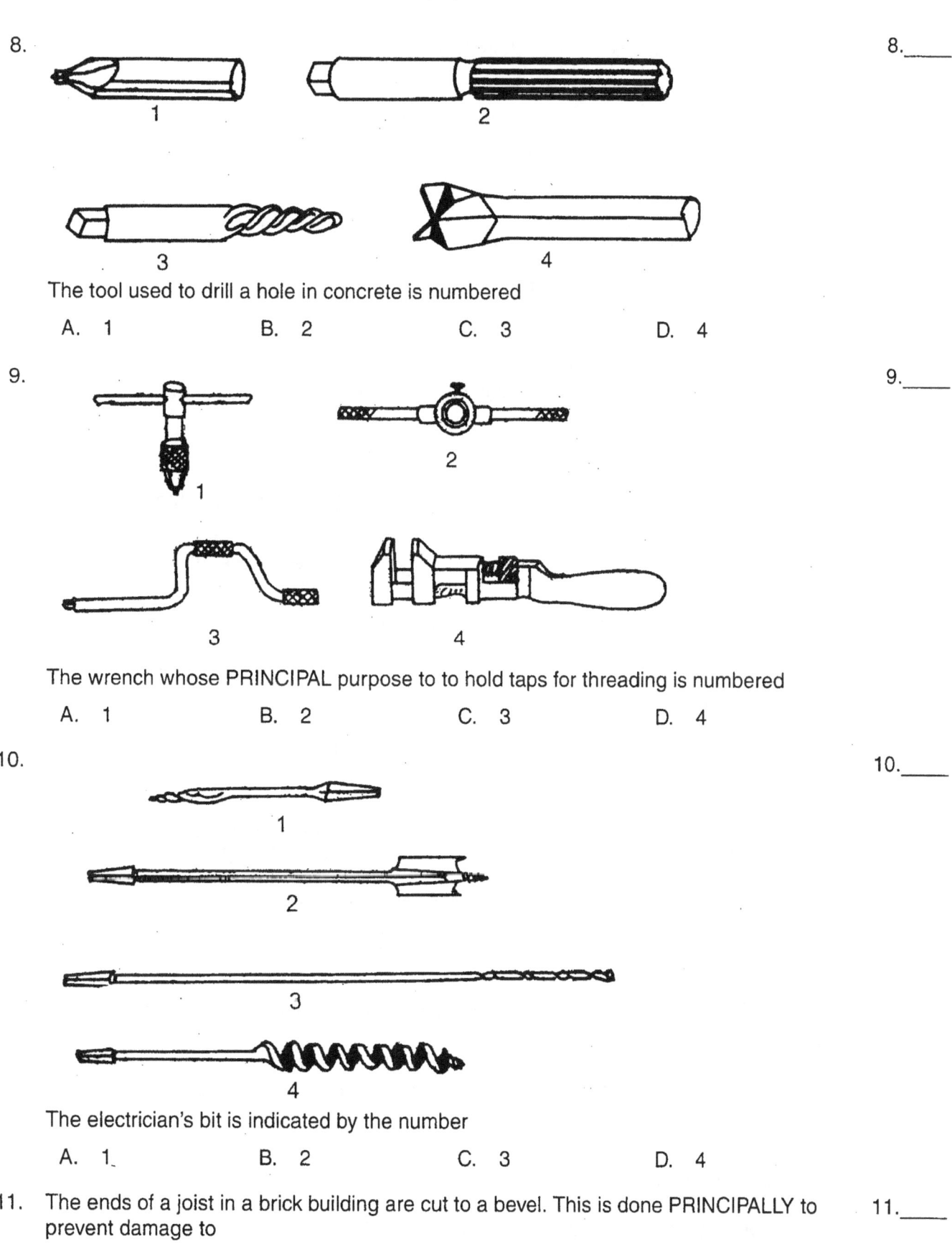

8. The tool used to drill a hole in concrete is numbered

   A. 1 B. 2 C. 3 D. 4

9. The wrench whose PRINCIPAL purpose to to hold taps for threading is numbered

   A. 1 B. 2 C. 3 D. 4

10. The electrician's bit is indicated by the number

    A. 1 B. 2 C. 3 D. 4

11. The ends of a joist in a brick building are cut to a bevel. This is done PRINCIPALLY to prevent damage to

    A. joist B. floor C. sill D. wall

12. Of the following, the wood that is MOST commonly used today for floor joists is

    A. long leaf yellow pine B. douglas fir
    C. oak D. birch

13. Quarter-sawed lumber is preferred for the BEST finished flooring PRINCIPALLY because it

    A. has the greatest strength B. shrinks the least
    C. is the easiest to nail D. is the easiest to handle

14. A tool used in hanging doors is a

    A. miter gauge B. line level
    C. try square D. butt gauge

15. Of the following, the MAXIMUM height that would be considered acceptable for a stair riser is

    A. 6 1/2" B. 7 1/2" C. 8 1/2" D. 9 1/2"

16. The PRINCIPAL reason for *cross banding* the layers of wood in a plywood panel is to _____ of the panel.

    A. reduce warping B. increase the strength
    C. reduce the cost D. increase the beauty

17. The part of a tree that will produce the DENSEST wood is the _____ wood.

    A. spring B. summer C. sap D. heart

18. Casing nails MOST NEARLY resemble _____ nails.

    A. common B. roofing C. form D. finishing

19. Lumber in quantity is ordered by

    A. cubic feet B. foot board measure
    C. lineal feet D. weight and length

20. For finishing of wood, BEST results are obtained by sanding

    A. with a circular motion
    B. against the grain
    C. with the grain
    D. with a circular motion on edges and against the grain on the flat parts

21. A *chase* in a brick wall is a

    A. pilaster B. waterstop C. recess D. corbel

22. Parging refers to

    A. increasing the thickness of a brick wall
    B. plastering the back of face brickwork
    C. bonding face brick to backing blocks
    D. leveling each course of brick

23. The PRINCIPAL reason for requiring brick to be wetted before laying is that 23.____

    A. less water is required in the mortar
    B. efflorescence is prevented
    C. the brick will not absorb as much water from the mortar
    D. cool brick is easier to handle

24. In brickwork, muriatic acid is commonly used to 24.____

    A. increase the strength of the mortar
    B. etch the brick
    C. waterproof the wall
    D. clean the wall

25. Cement mortar can be made easier to work by the addition of a small quantity of 25.____

    A. lime   B. soda   C. litharge   D. plaster

26. Headers in brickwork are used to _____ the wall. 26.____

    A. strengthen   B. reduce the cost of
    C. speed the erection of   D. align

27. Joints in brick walls are tooled 27.____

    A. immediately after each brick is laid
    B. after the mortar has had its initial set
    C. after the entire wall is completed
    D. 28 days after the wall has been built

28. If cement mortar has begun to set before it can be used in a wall, the BEST thing to do is to 28.____

    A. use the mortar immediately as is
    B. add a small quantity of lime
    C. add some water and mix thoroughly
    D. discard the mortar

29. A *bat* in brickwork is a 29.____

    A. brace to hold a wall temporarily in place
    B. stick used to aid in mixing of mortar
    C. broken piece of brick used to fill short spaces
    D. curved brick used in ornamental work

30. The proportions by volume of cement, lime, and sand in a cement-lime mortar should be, according to the Building Code, 30.____

    A. 1:1:3   B. 2:1:6   C. 1:1:6   D. 1:2:6

31. The BEST flux to use when soldering galvanized iron is 31.____

    A. killed acid   B. sal-ammoniac
    C. muriatic acid   D. resin

32. When soldering a vertical joint, the soldering iron should be tinned on _____ side(s).   32.____
    A. 1   B. 2   C. 3   D. 4

33. The difference between *right hand* and *left hand* tin snips is the   33.____
    A. relative position of the cutting jaws
    B. shape of the cutting jaws
    C. shape of the handles
    D. relative position of the handles

34. A machine used to bend sheet metal is called a   34.____
    A. router   B. planer   C. brake   D. swage

35. The type of solder that would be used in *hard soldering* would be _____ solder.   35.____
    A. bismuth   B. wiping   C. 50-50   D. silver

36. Roll roofing material is usually felt which has been impregnated with   36.____
    A. cement   B. mastic   C. tar   D. latex

37. The purpose of flashing on roofs is to   37.____
    A. secure roofing materials to the roof
    B. make it easier to lay the roofing
    C. prevent leaks through the roof
    D. insulate the roof from excessive heat

38. The tool used to spread hot pitch on a three-ply roofing job is a   38.____
    A. mop   B. spreader   C. pusher   D. broom

39. The cutting of glass can be facilitated by dipping the cutting wheel in   39.____
    A. *3-in-1* oil   B. water   C. lard   D. kerosene

40. The strips of metal used to hold glass to the window frame while it is being puttied are called   40.____
    A. hold-downs B. points   C. wedges   D. triangles

41. The type of chain used with sash weights is _____ link.   41.____
    A. flat   B. round
    C. figure-eight   D. basket-weave

42. The material that would be used to seal around a window frame is   42.____
    A. oakum   B. litharge   C. grout   D. calking

43. The function of a window sill is MOST NEARLY the same as that of a   43.____
    A. jamb   B. coping   C. lintel   D. brick

44. Lightweight plaster would be made with   44.____
    A. sand   B. cinders   C. potash   D. vermiculite

45. The FIRST coat of plaster to be applied on a three-coat plaster job is the _____ coat.   45.____
    A. brown   B. scratch   C. white   D. keene

46. Screeds in plaster work are used to   46.____
    A. remove larger sizes of sand
    B. hold the batch of plaster before it is applied
    C. apply the plaster to the wall
    D. guide the plasterer in making, an even wall

47. The FIRST coat of plaster over rock lath should be a _____ plaster.   47.____
    A. gypsum   B. lime
    C. portland cement   D. puzzolan cement

48. In plastering, a *hawk* is used to _____ plaster.   48.____
    A. apply   B. hold   C. scratch   D. smooth

49. When mixing concrete by hand, the order in which the ingredients should be mixed is: 49.____
    A. water, cement, sand, stone
    B. sand, cement, water, stone
    C. stone, water, sand, cement
    D. stone, sand, cement, water

50. The PRINCIPAL reason for covering a concrete sidewalk with straw or paper after the concrete has been poured is to   50.____
    A. prevent people from walking on the concrete while it is still wet
    B. impart a rough non-slip surface to the concrete
    C. prevent excessive evaporation of water in the concrete
    D. shorten the length of time it would take for the concrete to harden

KEY (CORRECT ANSWERS)

1. B	11. D	21. C	31. C	41. A
2. B	12. B	22. B	32. A	42. D
3. C	13. B	23. C	33. A	43. B
4. C	14. D	24. D	34. C	44. D
5. D	15. B	25. A	35. D	45. B
6. C	16. A	26. A	36. C	46. D
7. A	17. D	27. B	37. C	47. A
8. D	18. D	28. D	38. A	48. B
9. A	19. B	29. C	39. D	49. D
10. C	20. C	30. C	40. B	50. C

TEST 2

DIRECTIONS: Each question or incomplete statement is followed by several suggested answers or completions. Select the one that BEST answers the question or completes the statement. *PRINT THE LETTER OF THE CORRECT ANSWER IN THE SPACE AT THE RIGHT.*

1. When colored concrete is required, the colors used should be

    A. colors in oil
    B. mineral pigments
    C. tempera colors
    D. water colors

2. Concrete is *rubbed* with a(n)

    A. emery wheel
    B. carborundum brick
    C. sandstone
    D. alundum stick

3. To prevent concrete from sticking to forms, the forms should be painted with

    A. oil
    B. kerosene
    C. water
    D. lime

4. The reinforcement in a concrete floor slab is referred to as 6"-6" x #6-#6. The type of reinforcing that is being used is

    A. steel bars
    B. wire mesh
    C. angle irons
    D. grating plate

5. One method of measuring the consistency of a concrete mix is by means of a _____ test.

    A. penetration
    B. flow
    C. slump
    D. weight

6. A chemical that is sometimes used to prevent the freezing of concrete in cold weather is

    A. alum
    B. glycerine
    C. calcium chloride
    D. sodium nitrate

7. The one of the following that is LEAST commonly used for columns is

    A. wide flange beams
    B. angles
    C. concrete-filled pipe
    D. I beams

8. Fire protection of steel floor beams is MOST frequently accomplished by the use of

    A. gypsum block
    B. brick
    C. rock wool fill
    D. vermiculite gypsum plaster

9. A *Pittsburgh lock* is a(n)

    A. emergency door lock
    B. sheet metal joint
    C. elevator safety
    D. boiler valve

10. In order to drill a hole at right angle to the horizontal axis of a round bar, the bar should be held in a

    A. step block
    B. C-block
    C. hand pliers
    D. V-block

11. The procedure to follow in the lubrication of maintenance shop equipment is to lubricate 11.____

    A. when you can spare the time
    B. only when necessary
    C. at regular intervals
    D. when the equipment is in operation

12. Of the following items, the one which is NOT used in making fastenings to masonry or plaster walls is a(n) 12.____

    A. lead shield   B. expansion bolt
    C. rawl plug   D. steel bushing

13. When a common straight ladder is used to paint a wall, the safe distance that the foot of the ladder should be set away from the wall is MOST NEARLY _____ the length of the ladder. 13.____

    A. one-eighth   B. one-quarter
    C. one-half   D. five-eighths

14. The term *bell and spigot* usually refers to 14.____

    A. refrigerator motors   B. cast iron pipes
    C. steam radiator outlets D. electrical receptacles

15. In plumbing work, a valve which allows water to flow in one direction only is commonly known as a _____ valve. 15.____

    A. check   B. globe   C. gate   D. stop

16. A pipe coupling is BEST used to connect two pieces of pipe of 16.____

    A. the same diameter in a straight line
    B. the same diameter at right angles to each other
    C. different diameters at a 45° angle
    D. different diameters at an 1/8th bend

17. A fitting or pipe with many outlets relatively close together is commonly called a 17.____

    A. manifold   B. gooseneck
    C. flange union   D. return bend

18. To locate the center in the end of a sound shaft, the BEST tool to use is a(n) 18.____

    A. ruler   B. divider
    C. hermaphrodite caliper D. micrometer

19. When cutting a piece of 1 1/4" O.D. 20 gauge brass tubing with a hand hacksaw, it is BEST to use a blade having _____ teeth per inch. 19.____

    A. 14   B. 18   C. 22   D. 32

20. When cutting a piece of 1" O.D. extra-heavy pipe with a pipe cutter, a burr usually forms on the inside and the outside of the pipe. These burrs are BEST removed by means of a pipe 20.____

    A. tap and a file   B. wrench and rough stone
    C. reamer and a file   D. drill and a chisel

21. Artificial respiration should be started immediately on a man who has suffered an electric shock if he is

    A. *unconscious* and breathing
    B. *unconscious* and not breathing
    C. *conscious* and in a daze
    D. *conscious* and badly burned

22. The fuse of a certain circuit has blown and is replaced with a fuse of the same rating which also blows when the switch is closed.
    In this case,

    A. a fuse of higher current rating should be used
    B. a fuse of higher voltage rating should be used
    C. the fuse should be temporarily replaced by a heavy piece of wire
    D. the circuit should be checked

23. Operating an incandescent electric light bulb at less than its rated voltage will result in

    A. shorter life and brighter light
    B. longer life and dimmer light
    C. brighter light and longer life
    D. dimmer light and shorter life

24. In order to control a lamp from two different positions, it is necessary to use

    A. two single pole switches
    B. one single pole switch and one four-way switch
    C. two three-way switches
    D. one single pole switch and one four-way switch

25.

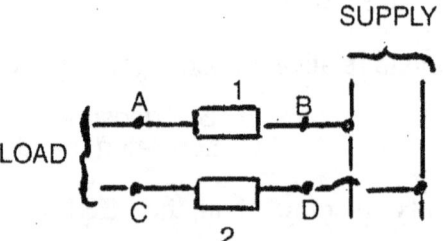

One method of testing fuses is to connect a pair of test lamps in the circuit in such a manner that the test lamp will light up if the fuse is good and will remain dark if the fuse is bad. In the above illustration 1 and 2 are fuses.
In order to test if fuse 1 is bad, test lamps should be connected between

    A. A and B   B. B and D   C. A and D   D. C and B

26. The PRINCIPAL reason for the grounding of electrical equipment and circuits is to

    A. prevent short circuits   B. insure safety from shock
    C. save power   D. increase voltage

27. The ordinary single-pole flush wall type switch must be connected

    A. across the line
    B. in the *hot* conductor
    C. in the grounded conductor
    D. in the white conductor

28. A D.C. shunt motor runs in the wrong direction. This fault can be CORRECTED by

    A. reversing the connections of both the field and the armature
    B. interchanging the connections of either main or auxiliar windings
    C. interchanging the connections to either the field or the armature windings
    D. interchanging the connections to the line of the power leads

29. The MOST common type of motor that can be used with both A.C. and D.C. sources is the _____ motor.

    A. compound   B. repulsion   C. series   D. shunt

30. A fluorescent fixture in a new building has been in use for several months without trouble. Recently, the ends of the fluorscent lamp have remained lighted when the light was switched off.
    The BEST way to clear up this trouble is to replace the

    A. lamp   B. ballast   C. starter   D. sockets

31. The BEST wood to use for handles of tools such as axes and hammers is

    A. hemlock   B. pine   C. oak   D. hickory

32. A *hanger bolt*

    A. has a square head
    B. is bent in a *U* shape
    C. has a different type of thread at each end
    D. is threaded the entire length from point to head

33. A stone frequently used to sharpen tools is

    A. carborundum   B. bauxite   C. resin   D. slate

34. A strike plate is MOST closely associated with a

    A. lock   B. sash   C. butt   D. tie rod

35. The material that distinguishes a terrazzo floor from an ordinary concrete floor is

    A. cinders
    B. marble chip
    C. cut stone
    D. non-slip aggregate

36. A room is 7'6" wide by 9'0" long with a ceiling height of 8'0". One gallon of flat paint will cover approximately 400 square feet of wall.
    The number of gallons of this paint required to paint the walls of this room, making no deductions for windows or doors, is MOST NEARLY _____ gallon.

    A. 1/4   B. 1/2   C. 3/4   D. 1

37. The cost of a certain job is broken down as follows:
    Materials $375
    Rental of equipment 120
    Labor   315
    The percentage of the total cost of the job that can be charged to materials is MOST NEARLY

    A. 40%   B. 42%   C. 44%   D. 46%

38. By trial, it is found that by using two cubic feet of sand, a five cubic foot batch of concrete is produced.
    Using the same proportions, the amount of sand required to produce 2 cubic yards of concrete is MOST NEARLY _____ cu.ft.

    A. 20   B. 22   C. 24   D. 26

39. It takes 4 men 6 days to do a certain job.
    Working at the same speed, the number of days it will take 3 men to do this job is

    A. 7   B. 8   C. 9   D. 10

40. The cost of rawl plugs is $2.75 per gross. The cost of 2,448 rawl plugs is

    A. $46.75   B. $47.25   C. $47.75   D. $48.25

41. *Rigidity* of the hammer handle enables the operator to control and direct the force of the blow.
    As used above, *rigidity* means MOST NEARLY

    A. straightness   B. strength
    C. shape   D. stiffness

42. *For precision work, center punches are ground to a fine tapered point.* As used above, *tapered* means MOST NEARLY

    A. conical   B. straight   C. accurate   D. smooth

43. *There are limitations to the drilling of metals by hand power.*
    As used above, *limitations* means MOST NEARLY

    A. advantages   B. restrictions
    C. difficulties   D. benefits

Questions 44-45.

DIRECTIONS: Questions 44 and 45 are based on the following paragraph.

Because electric drills run at high speed, the cutting edges of a twist drill are heated quickly. If the metal is thick, the drill point must be withdrawn from the hole frequently to cool it and clear out chips. Forcing the drill continuously into a deep hole will heat it, thereby spoiling its temper and cutting edges. A portable electric drill has the advantage that it can be taken to the work and used to drill holes in material too large to handle in a drill press.

44. According to the above paragraph, overheating of a twist drill will

    A. slow down the work   B. cause excessive drill breakage
    C. dull the drill   D. spoil the accuracy of the work

45. According to the above paragraph, one method of preventing overheating of a twist drill is to

    A. use cooling oil
    B. drill a smaller pilot hole first
    C. use a drill press
    D. remove the drill from the work frequently

Questions 46-50.

DIRECTIONS: Questions 46 to 50 are to be answered in accordance with the sketch shown below.

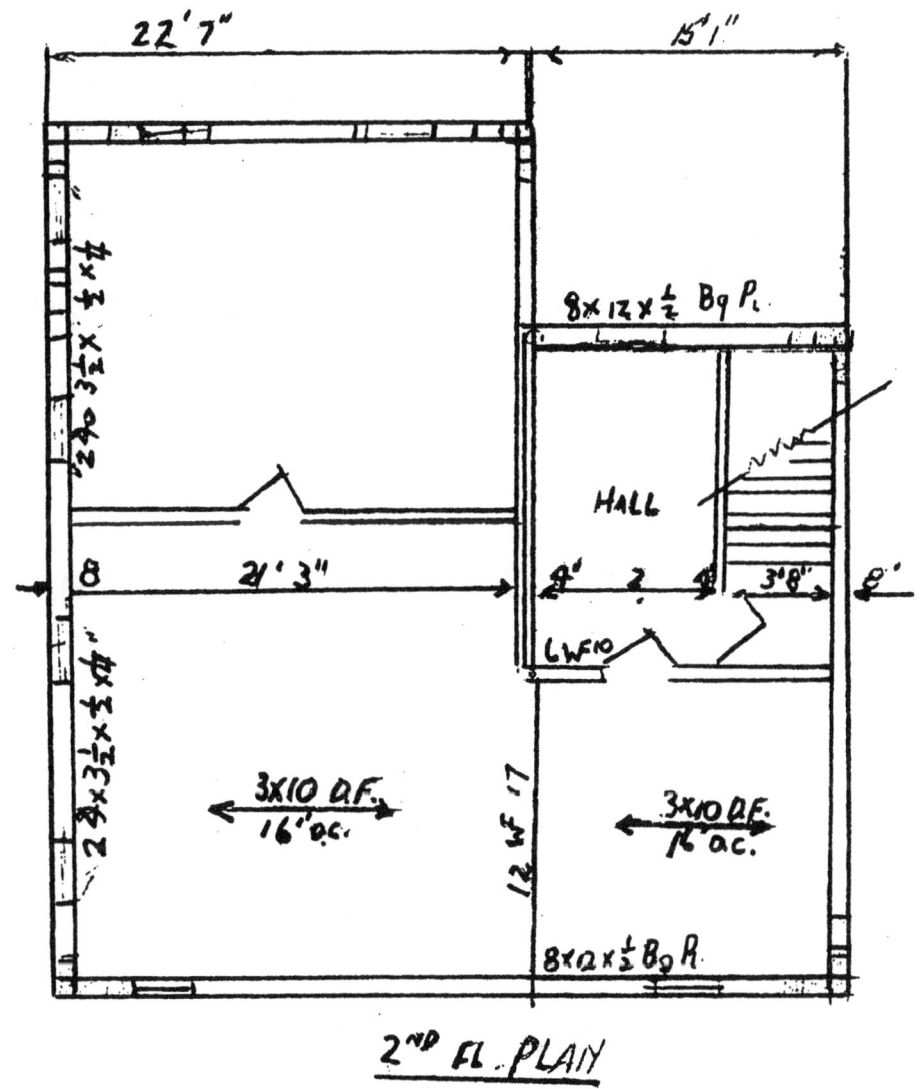

2ND FL. PLAN

46. The one of the following statements that is CORRECT is the building

    A. is of fireproof construction
    B. has masonry walls with wood joists
    C. is of wood frame construction
    D. has timber joists and girders

47. The one of the following statements that is CORRECT is 47.___

    A. the stairway from the ground continues through the roof
    B. there are two means of egress from the second floor of this building
    C. the door on the second floor stair landing opens in the direction of egress
    D. the entire stair is shown on this plan

48. The width of the hall is 48.___

    A. 10'3"   B. 10'5"   C. 10'7"   D. 10'9"

49. The lintels shown are 49.___

    A. angles   B. a channel and an angle
    C. an I-beam   D. precast concrete

50. The one of the following statements that is CORRECT is that the steel beam is 50.___

    A. supported by columns at the center and at the ends
    B. entirely supported by the walls
    C. supported on columns at the ends only
    D. supported at the center by a column and at the ends by the walls

KEY (CORRECT ANSWERS)

1. B	11. C	21. B	31. D	41. D
2. B	12. D	22. D	32. C	42. A
3. A	13. B	23. B	33. A	43. B
4. B	14. B	24. C	34. A	44. C
5. C	15. A	25. C	35. B	45. D
6. C	16. A	26. B	36. C	46. B
7. B	17. A	27. B	37. D	47. C
8. D	18. C	28. C	38. B	48. D
9. B	19. D	29. C	39. B	49. A
10. D	20. C	30. C	40. A	50. D

EXAMINATION SECTION
TEST 1

DIRECTIONS: Each question or incomplete statement is followed by several suggested answers or completions. Select the one that BEST answers the question or completes the statement. *PRINT THE LETTER OF THE CORRECT ANSWER IN THE SPACE AT THE RIGHT.*

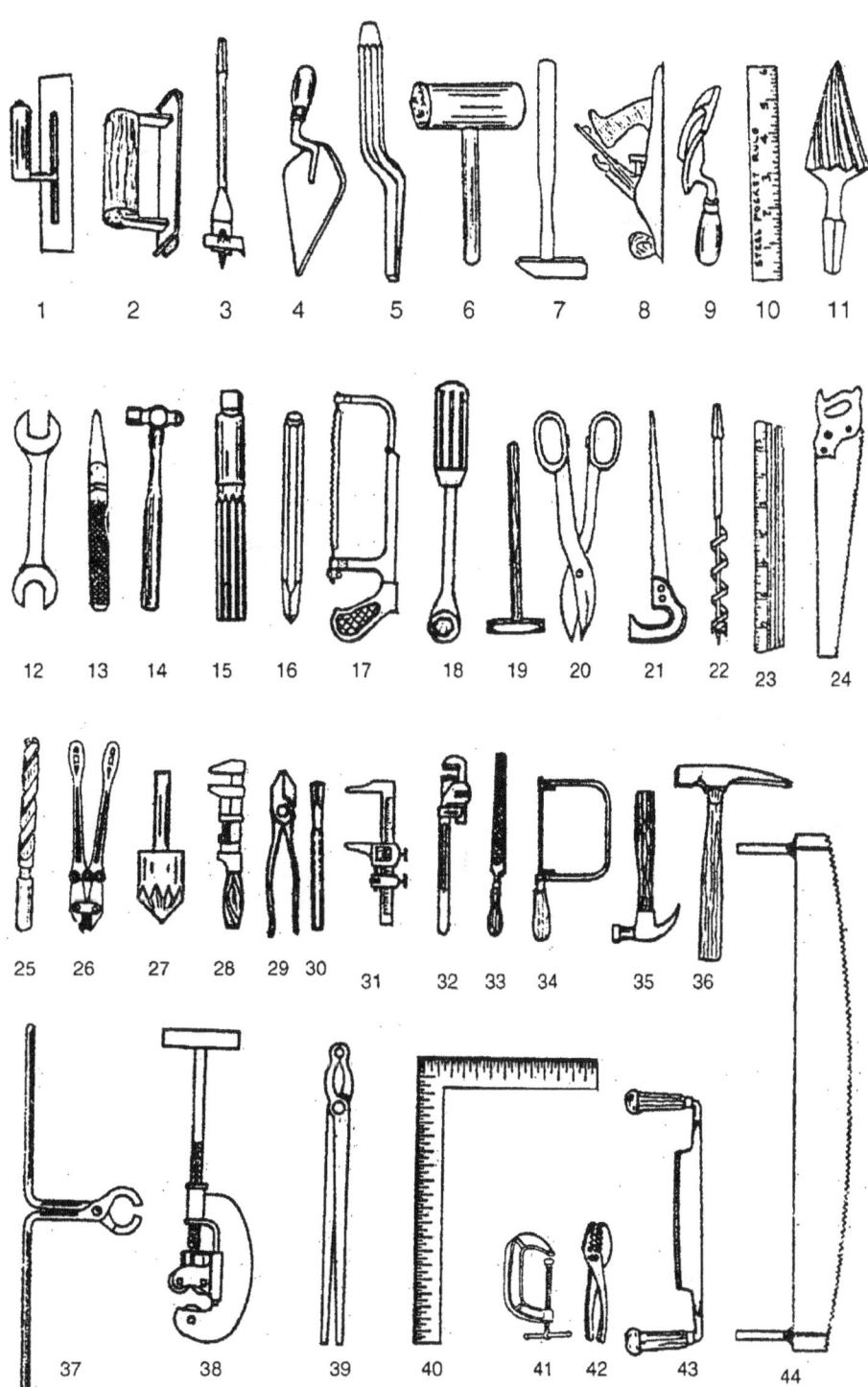

1. Of the following, which group of three tools is used *most nearly* in the same way?

    A. Tools 4, 21, 39
    B. Tools 11, 16, 42
    C. Tools 14, 35, 36
    D. Tools 5, 6, 13

2. If you want to cut a disc out of sheet metal, you should use tool no.

    A. 20 B. 26 C. 29 D. 38

3. Tool number 25 is ordinarily NOT used alone; it should be used with tool no.

    A. 28
    B. 35
    C. 39
    D. another tool not pictured

4. To split a brick in half you should FIRST chip the line of division all the way around the brick with tool no.

    A. 14 B. 24 C. 34 D. 36

5. To repair wide cracks in a wood floor you should glue a thin strip of wood into the crack and then level it even with the surrounding floor surface. To level this strip of wood you should use tool no.

    A. 1 B. 8 C. 24 D. 33

6. To smooth a newly laid concrete surface so that it is free of ripples and marks, you should use tool no.

    A. 1 B. 6 C. 8 D. 9

7. To measure the *outside* diameter of a section of pipe MOST accurately, the tool that should be used is tool no.

    A. 10 B. 23 C. 31 D. 40

8. The BEST tool to use to cut a curved pattern in a 1/4 inch-thick sheet of plywood is tool no.

    A. 17 B. 24 C. 34 D. 43

9. If you, as a member of a repair crew, plan to cut a rectangular piece of plywood measuring 18" x 12" out of a larger rectangular piece measuring 30" x 24", the tool that will BEST help lay out the lines and check the angles is number

    A. 10 B. 23 C. 31 D. 40

10. Either end of tool 12 can be *properly* used for the purpose of

    A. fitting into the handle of another tool
    B. turning nuts or bolts
    C. laying out angles
    D. pulling nails

11. Tools 22, 24, 35 and 40 have in common that fact that they are used *primarily* in

    A. masonry
    B. plumbing
    C. sheet metal work
    D. woodworking

12. Which tool requires the use of BOTH hands on the tool to operate it properly? 12.____

    A. Tool 8   B. Tool 12   C. Tool 20   D. Tool 24

13. Of the following, the tool designed to be used for turning nuts of various sizes is tool no. 13.____

    A. 19   B. 28   C. 29   D. 31

14. To cut a section of pipe to the required length, the MOST appropriate tool is number 14.____

    A. 20   B. 29   C. 31   D. 38

15. In the picture below of a roof, which one of the numbered arrows points to the "flashing"? 15.____

    A. 1   B. 2   C. 3   D. 4

16. The function of glazier's points is to 16.____

    A. keep the putty from dirtying the glass
    B. make it easy to cut glass in a straight line
    C. hold a pane of glass in place
    D. aid in applying putty evenly around the glass

17. It is *desirable* for a putty knife used for patching plaster cracks to be flexible because a flexible putty knife 17.____

    A. makes it difficult for the user to cut his hands while applying the plaster
    B. is easier to keep clean than one made of rigid material
    C. can press the patching materials into the crack, filling it completely
    D. makes it possible to pick up the exact amount of plaster required

18. Using a fuse with a *larger* rated capacity than that of the circuit is 18.____

    A. *advisable;* such use prevents the fuse from blowing
    B. *advisable;* larger capacity fuses last longer than smaller capacity fuses
    C. *inadvisable;* larger capacity fuses are more expensive than smaller capacity fuses
    D. *inadvisable;* such use may cause a fire

19. You can MOST easily tell when a screw-in type fuse has blown because the center of the strip of metal in the fuse is 19.____

    A. broken   B. visible
    C. nicked   D. cool to the touch

20. In the picture below, which of the numbered arrows points to the door "jamb?" 20.____

    A. 1   B. 2   C. 3   D. 4

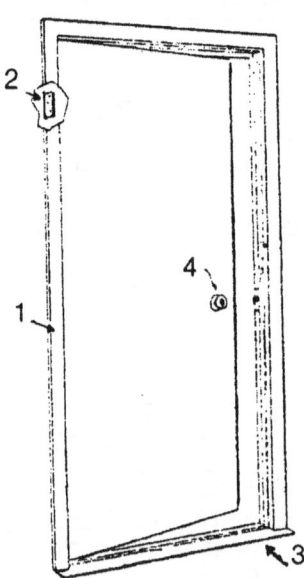

21. Of the following, the MAIN reason why flashing is used in the building trade is to make an area 21.____

    A. decorative   B. watertight   C. level   D. heat-resistant

22. To prepare a ready-mixed concrete material for use, you FIRST add 22.____

    A. gravel   B. salt   C. sand   D. water

23. When working on wet floors with an electrically powered tool, additional safety against electric shock can BEST be provided by 23.____

    A. a longer electric cord   B. an AC-DC converter
    C. rubber gloves   D. loose clothing

24. Which one of the wrenches pictured below is designed to grip round pipes in making plumbing repairs? 24.____

    A. 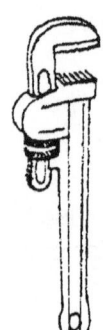   B.    C.    D.

25. Which one of the saws pictured below would be BEST to use to cut steel bar stock?   25.____

    A.   B.
    C.   D.

26. Which one of the hammers pictured below is a claw hammer?   26.____

    A.   B.   C.   D.

27. The terms "dovetail" and "dowel" are used to describe types of   27.____

    A. glues   B. joints   C. clamps   D. tile

28. A three-prong plug on a power tool used on a 120-volt line indicates that the tool   28.____

    A. may be grounded against electric shock
    B. is provided with additional power through the third prong
    C. has a defect and should be returned
    D. is adaptable for use with AC or DC current

29. A bit and brace should be used to   29.____

    A. saw wood   B. glue wood
    C. drill holes   D. support or hold work

30. Which of the following would ordinarily occur FIRST in a toilet tank after the handle is pushed down to flush the toilet?   30.____

    A. Float ball drops with water level, opening the ballcock assembly through which fresh water flows into the tank
    B. Tank ball sinks slowly into place
    C. Rising water pushes the float ball up until it closes the ballcock assembly, shutting off the supply of fresh water when the tank is full
    D. The tank ball lifts, opening the outlet so water can flow from tank to bowl

KEY (CORRECT ANSWERS)

1. C
2. A
3. D
4. D
5. B

6. A
7. C
8. C
9. D
10. B

11. D
12. A
13. B
14. D
15. B

16. C
17. C
18. D
19. A
20. A

21. B
22. D
23. C
24. A
25. B

26. C
27. B
28. A
29. C
30. D

TEST 2

DIRECTIONS: Each question or incomplete statement is followed by several suggested answers or completions. Select the one that BEST answers the question or completes the statement. *PRINT THE LETTER OF THE CORRECT ANSWER IN THE SPACE AT THE RIGHT.*

1. Of the following, the MAIN reason for clear glass doors to have a painted design about four and one-half feet above the floor is to

    A. look attractive
    B. prevent glare
    C. improve safety
    D. make damage, if any, less noticeable

    1.____

2. When using a wrench to make a repair on a faucet, it is a good idea to cover the wrench with rags in order to

    A. protect the finish on the faucet
    B. get a closer fit over the faucet
    C. get a better grip on the wrench
    D. get a better grip on the faucet

    2.____

3. The length of the screw in the sketch below is *most nearly*

    A. 1 7/8"   B. 2"   C. 2 1/4"   D. 2 5/16"

    3.____

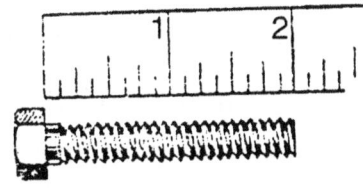

4. Panel doors may have horns which must be cut off before the door is hung. In the sketch below, the arrow which indicates a horn is labeled number

    A. 1   B. 2   C. 3   D. 4

    4.____

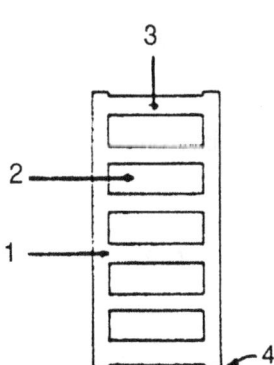

5. To "shim a hinge" means to

   A. swing the hinge from side to side
   B. paint the hinge
   C. polish the hinge
   D. raise up the hinge

6. To hold work that is being planed, sawed, drilled, shaped, sharpened or riveted, you should use a

   A. punch   B. rasp   C. reamer   D. vise

7. A good deal of the trouble caused by faulty and worn locks and hinges can be avoided by proper lubrication.
   The tool you would use to lubricate locks and hinges is

   A.   B.   C.   D.

8. The terms ALLIGATORING, BLISTERING, and PEELING refer to

   A. carpentry   B. masonry   C. painting   D. plumbing

9. The terms BAT and STRETCHER refer to

   A. carpentry   B. glazing   C. masonry   D. painting

10. Ladders which are used to extend as high as 60 feet are called

    A. extension ladders
    B. portable ladders
    C. single-section ladders
    D. stepladders

11. Of the following, the MOST important advantage that Plexiglass has over regular glass, when used in windows, is that it

    A. is available in a wide range of thicknesses
    B. is easier to clean
    C. offers greater resistance to breakage
    D. offers greater resistance to scratches

12. Clutch-head, offset, Phillips and spiral-ratchet all are different types of

    A. drills   B. files   C. wrenches   D. screwdrivers

13. Of the following, the MOST important reason for keeping tools in perfect working order is to make sure

    A. the proper tool is being used for the required work
    B. the tools can be operated safely
    C. each employee can repair a variety of building defects
    D. no employee uses a tool for his private use

14. When repairing a hole in a leaking pipe which of the following should be done FIRST? 14.____

    A. Wrap tape around the hole
    B. Turn off the water supply
    C. Tighten a clamp around the hole
    D. Seal the hole with epoxy

15. Freshly cut threads on pipe should be handled with caution *mainly* because the threads 15.____

    A. are the weakest section of the pipe and break easily
    B. do not give a firm handhold for carrying
    C. make a tight seal around a joint
    D. are always sharp

16. When a repair worker must enter a confined space through a small opening, it is a GOOD idea to attach a rope to his body *mainly* because the 16.____

    A. rope reduces unnecessary strain on the body
    B. rope may provide a way to reach the worker in an emergency
    C. worker will be able to get to areas that are not easily reached
    D. worker may be able to use the rope to remove debris from the work space

17. Hitting the handle of a screw driver with a hammer to remove an imbedded screw is a 17.____

    A. *good* practice, since it supplies the necessary force to get the screw started
    B. *poor* practice, since the shank part of the screw driver can be bent and the tool made useless
    C. *good* practice, since hammers and screw drivers are available in every tool kit just for this purpose
    D. *poor* practice, since the blade tip of the screw driver cannot be guided into the screw slot when both hands are holding the tools

18. Of the following, the reason why a tank, such as that pictured below, that is otherwise working correctly might fail to fill up sufficiently to deliver enough water to the toilet bowl at the time it is needed is that the 18.____

    A. ball may not drop back over the valve seat
    B. excess water may be flowing into the drain
    C. float rod may be bent up
    D. valve seat may be worn or nicked

19. In the sketch below, the measurement of the inside diameter is *most nearly* _____ inches.

    A. 24   B. 3   C. 3 1/2   D. 4

20. In a two-wire electrical system, the color of the wire which is grounded is *usually*

    A. white   B. red   C. black   D. green

21. It is generally recommended that wooden ladders be kept coated with a suitable protective coating.
    The one of the following which is NOT a suitable protective coating is

    A. clear lacquer   B. clear varnish
    C. linseed oil   D. paint

22. The tool you should use to mend metal by soldering is

    A.   B.   C.   D.

23. Of the following, the MOST effective method of fixing a door that sticks is to locate the area of the door which sticks and then to _____ it.

    A. lacquer   B. plane   C. tape   D. varnish

24. Which one of the following should be used to thin latex paint?

    A. Mineral spirits   B. Turpentine
    C. Denatured alcohol   D. Water

25. Of the following, the MAIN reason you should NOT place a ladder directly in front of a door that opens toward the ladder is that   25._____

    A. there is not enough space to support the weight of the ladder
    B. you would have to step down off the ladder each time someone wants to use the door
    C. this would prove to be hazardous if someone comes through the door
    D. it would be hard to reach the areas that need repair without tipping the ladder off balance

26. Going over the cutting line MORE than once when cutting a pane of glass by hand with a cutting wheel is *usually*   26._____

    A. *advisable;* it gives a straighter line
    B. *advisable;* it gives a cleaner break
    C. *inadvisable;* it gives an uneven break
    D. *inadvisable;* it may blunt the edge of the glass cutter

27. When hammering, it is usually BEST to hold the handle of the hammer   27._____

    A. close to the head because this maximizes the force of the blow
    B. far away from the head because this maximizes the force of the blow
    C. close to the head because this reduces the force of the blow
    D. far away from the head because this reduces the force of the blow

28. Repair crew members should report accidents on the job IMMEDIATELY *primarily* so that   28._____

    A. the proper person will be reprimanded for his carelessness
    B. a correct count can be kept of time lost through accidents
    C. prompt medical care may be given when needed
    D. the correct forms will be filled out

29. Leather gloves should be worn when handling sheet metal *primarily* because   29._____

    A. pressure on the metal might cause it to bend
    B. the edges and corners of the metal may be sharp
    C. natural oil or moisture from hands corrodes the metal
    D. leather provides a more secure grip

30. If a portable ladder does NOT have a nonslip base, the way to overcome this deficiency so that the ladder can be used safely is to   30._____

    A. place the ladder on soft earth
    B. fasten a wooden board across the top of the ladder
    C. splice two short ladders together
    D. tie the bottom of the ladder to a secure structure

KEY (CORRECT ANSWERS)

1.	C	16.	B
2.	A	17.	B
3.	B	18.	A
4.	D	19.	B
5.	D	20.	A
6.	D	21.	D
7.	B	22.	B
8.	C	23.	B
9.	C	24.	D
10.	A	25.	C
11.	C	26.	C
12.	D	27.	B
13.	B	28.	C
14.	B	29.	B
15.	D	30.	D

EXAMINATION SECTION
TEST 1

DIRECTIONS: Each question or incomplete statement is followed by several suggested answers or completions. Select the one that BEST answers the question or completes the statement. *PRINT THE LETTER OF THE CORRECT ANSWEE IN THE SPACE AT THE RIGHT.*

1. As a member of a repair crew, you have been asked by your supervisor to reinforce a door. You have never done this kind of work before and are not certain how to go about it. Of the following, the MOST advisable action to take is to

    A. tell your supervisor you need assistance
    B. ask the other crew members if they can help you
    C. go ahead and do the best you can
    D. ask another member of your crew if he will do it for you

    1._____

2. It is BEST to erect a barricade or barrier before repair work begins *mainly* because

    A. the repair truck can be sent back for additional supplies
    B. the workers can work in more comfortable space
    C. unauthorized persons are kept clear of the work area
    D. a solid platform is provided for workers' use

    2._____

3. Of the following, the BEST reason for sprinkling water on work areas which have a lot of dust or where the work itself will create a lot of dust is that this action will

    A. dissolve the dust particles
    B. help the dust to settle
    C. clean away the dust from the area
    D. prevent the dust from drying out

    3._____

QUESTIONS 4-9.
Questions 4 through 9 are to be answered *solely* on the basis of the following set of instructions.

Patching Simple Cracks in a Built-Up Roof

If there is a visible crack in built-up roofing, the repair is simple and straight forward:
1. With a brush, clean all loose gravel and dust out of the crack, and clean three or four inches around all sides of it.
2. With a trowel or putty knife, fill the crack with asphalt cement and then spread a layer of asphalt cement about 1/8 inch thick over the cleaned area.
3. Place a strip of roofing felt big enough to cover the crack into the wet cement and press it down firmly.
4. Spread a second layer of cement over the strip of felt and well past its edges.
5. Brush gravel back over the patch.

4. According to the above passage, in order to patch simple cracks in a built-up roof, it is necessary to use a

    A. putty knife and a drill   B. knife and pliers
    C. tack hammer and a punch   D. brush and a trowe

    4._____

5. According to the above passage, the size of the area that should be clear of loose gravel and dust before the asphalt cement is first applied should

    A. be the exact size of the crack itself
    B. extend three or four inches on all sides of the crack
    C. be 1/8 inch greater than the size of the crack itself
    D. extend the length of the roofing strip

6. According to the above passage, loose gravel and dust in the crack should be removed with a

    A. brush   B. felt pad   C. trowel   D. dust mop

7. Assume that both layers of asphalt cement needed to patch the crack are of the same thickness.
The total thickness of asphalt cement used in the patch should be, *most nearly*, _____ inch.

    A. 1/2   B. 1/3   C. 1/4   D. 1/8

8. According to the instructions in the above passage, how large should the strip of roofing felt be cut?

    A. Three of four inches square
    B. Smaller than the crack and small enough to be surrounded by cement on all sides of the strip
    C. Exactly the same size and shape of the area covered by the wet cement
    D. Large enough to completely cover the crack

9. The final or finishing action to be taken in patching a simple crack in a built-up roof is to

    A. clean out the inside of the crack
    B. spread a layer of asphalt a second time
    C. cover the crack with roofing felt
    D. cover the patch of roofing felt and cement with gravel

10. As a repair crew worker, your supervisor tells you that he has in the workshop a piece of glass measuring 5' x 4' from which he wants you to cut a section measuring 4'8" x 3'2". However, you find two pieces of glass in the workshop; one is 5' x 3', and the other is 8' x 5'.
Of the following, the BEST action for you to take is to

    A. cut a section measuring 4'8" x 3' from the smaller piece because that is probably what he meant
    B. do NOT cut the glass and wait until he asks you for it
    C. tell him about the differences in measurement and ask him what to do
    D. cut a section measuring 4'8" x 3'2" from the larger piece since that would give you the full size required

11. A floor that is 9' wide by 12' long measures how many square feet?

    A. 12   B. 21   C. 108   D. 150

12. The sum of 5 1/16, 4 1/4, 4 3/8, and 3 7/16 is   12._____

    A. 17 1/8   B. 17 7/16   C. 17 1/4   D. 17 3/8

13. From a length of pipe 6 feet 9 inches long you are asked to cut a piece 4 feet 5 inches   13._____
    long.
    The length of the remainder, in inches, should be

    A. 24   B. 26   C. 28   D. 53

QUESTIONS 14-17.
In answering questions 14 through 17 refer to the label pictured below.

LABEL

BREGSON'S CLEAR GLUE HIGHLY FLAMMABLE	PRECAUTIONS
A clear quick-drying glue	Use with adequate ventilation
For temporary bonding, apply glue to one surface and join immediately	Close container after use
For permanent bonding, apply glue to both surfaces, permit to dry and press together	Keep out of reach of children
Use for bonding plastic to plastic, plastic to wood, and wood to wood only	Avoid prolonged breathing of vapors and repeated contact with skin
Will not bond at temperatures below 60°	

14. Assume that you, as a member of a repair crew, have been asked to repair a wood banister in the hallway of a house. Since the heat has been turned off, the hallway is very cold, except for the location where you have to make the repair. Another repair crew worker is working at that same location using a blow torch to solder a pipe in the wall.   14._____

    The temperature at that location is about 67°.
    According to the instruction on the above label, the use of this glue to make the necessary repair is

    A. *advisable;* the glue will bond wood to wood
    B. *advisable;* the heat form the soldering will cause the glue to dry quickly
    C. *inadvisable;* the work area temperature is too low
    D. *inadvisable;* the glue is highly flammable

15. According to the instructions on the above label, this glue should NOT be used for which of the following applications?   15._____

    A. Affixing a pine table leg to a walnut table
    B. Repairing leaks around pipe joints
    C. Bonding a plastic knob to a cedar drawer
    D. Attaching a lucite knob to a lucite drawer

16. According to the instructions on the above label, using this glue to bond ceramic tile to a plaster wall by coating both surfaces with glue, letting the glue dry, and then pressing the tile to the plaster wall is

    A. *advisable;* the glue is quick drying and clear
    B. *advisable;* the glue should be permanently affixed to the one surface of the tile only
    C. *inadvisable;* the glue is not suitable for bonding ceramic tile to plaster walls
    D. *inadvisable;* the bonding should be a temporary one

17. The precaution described in the above label "use with adequate ventilation" means that

    A. the area you are working in should be very cold
    B. there should be sufficient fresh air where you are using the glue
    C. you should wear gloves to avoid contact with the glue
    D. you must apply a lot of glue to make a permanent bond

QUESTIONS 18-20.
Questions 18 through 20 are to be answered *solely* on the basis of the following passage.

A utility plan is a floor plan which shows the layout of a heating, electrical, plumbing, or other utility system. Utility plans are used primarily by the persons responsible for the utilities, but they are important to the craftsman as well. Most utility installations require the leaving of openings in walls, floors, and roofs for the admission or installation of utility features. The craftsman who is, for example, pouring a concrete foundation wall must study the utility plans to determine the number, sizes, and locations of the openings he must leave for piping, electric lines, and the like.

18. The one of the following items of information which is LEAST likely to be provided by a utility plan is the

    A. location of the joists and frame members around
    B. stairwells
    C. location of the hot water supply and return piping
    D. location of light fixtures D. number of openings in the floor for radiators

19. According to the passage, the persons who will *most likely* have the GREATEST need for the information included in a utility plan of a building are those who

    A. maintain and repair the heating system
    B. clean the premises
    C. paint housing exteriors
    D. advertise property for sale

20. According to the passage, a repair crew member should find it MOST helpful to consult a utility plan when information is needed about the

    A. thickness of all doors in the structure
    B. number of electrical outlets located throughout the structure
    C. dimensions of each window in the structure
    D. length of a roof rafter

KEY (CORRECT ANSWERS)

1.	A	11.	C
2.	C	12.	A
3.	B	13.	C
4.	D	14.	D
5.	B	15.	B
6.	A	16.	C
7.	C	17.	B
8.	D	18.	A
9.	D	19.	A
10.	C	20.	B

TEST 2

DIRECTIONS: Each question or incomplete statement is followed by several suggested answers or completions. Select the one that BEST answers the question or completes the statement. *PRINT THE LETTER OF THE CORRECT ANSWER IN THE SPACE AT THE RIGHT.*

1. Repair crew men should report accidents on the job IMMEDIATELY *primarily* so that   1.___

    A. the proper person will be reprimanded for his carelessness
    B. a correct count can be kept of time lost through accidents on the job
    C. prompt medical care may be given when needed
    D. the correct forms will be filled out

2. In a circulating hot-water heating system, most boilers have an altitude gauge that shows the level of the water in the system. This gauge has two needles, one red, which is set at the proper water level, and one black, which shows the true water level, and which varies with the water-level change. When the red needle is over the black on the gauge, so that they coincide, it means that the system   2.___

    A. has too much water
    B. requires more water
    C. is properly filled with water
    D. should be shut off

3. If a radiator fails to heat properly, the FIRST of the following actions which you should take is to check the   3.___

    A. boiler's steam gauge   B. boiler's water line
    C. radiator's shut-off valve   D. pressure reducing valve

4. Assume that you have been asked to remove a door knob. You inspect the door and find that it has a mortise lock, and that the door knob is fastened with a set screw.   4.___
Which of the following is the FIRST step that you should take in removing the door knob?

    A. Unscrew the set screw on the slimmest part of the knob
    B. Saw off the knob at its thinnest point
    C. Turn the knob repeatedly to the right and to the left until it finally falls off
    D. Use a pinchbar to spring the lock

5. When preparing a 1:1:6 mix for mortar, how many pails of lime should be added to 3 pails of sand and 1/2 pail of cement?   5.___

    A. 3   B. 1   C. 1/2   D. 1/4

6. If you find that the putty in the can is a little too hard to use, you should add some   6.___

    A. whiting   B. linseed oil
    C. spackle   D. glazing compound

7. The purpose of scratching the surface of the first coat of patching stucco is to 7.____

    A. spread the patching stucco over a wide area
    B. give the surface a textured finish
    C. provide a gripping surface for the next coat of patching stucco
    D. press the patching stucco into the hole to be repaired

8. When filling in large cracks and holes up to 2 inches in diameter in plaster walls it is BEST to use 8.____

    A. spackle
    B. patching plaster
    C. gypsum wallboard
    D. tile

9. Of the following, the MAIN reason for having a vertical distance of about 7 inches between stair treads is that this 9.____

    A. makes for the best appearance
    B. makes an easy step for the average person
    C. allows for the most profitable use of wood
    D. cuts out a good deal of unnecessary work

10. When removing a door from its hinges to make repairs, it is ALWAYS best to 10.____

    A. remove the pin from the top hinge first
    B. keep the door tightly closed
    C. remove the pin from the bottom hinge first
    D. remove the door knob and lock

11. Dry plaster will absorb water from the patching material, weakening and shrinking it. Based on the information in this statement, it would be *advisable* to take which one of the following actions in the process of patching a plaster crack? 11.____

    A. Mix the plaster with a lot of extra water
    B. Apply water-eased paint to the wall immediately
    C. Apply plaster powder to the crack, then pour water in over it
    D. Dampen the area surrounding the patch with a sponge

12. Standard electrical tools which are safe for ordinary use may be unsafe in locations which contain flammable materials because 12.____

    A. there may be insufficient ventilation
    B. sparks from the tools may start a fire
    C. electric current will usually cause fire
    D. the automatic sprinkler system may be set off accidentally

13. Of the following, the BEST combination of ingredients to use for good concrete is 13.____

    A. cement and water
    B. aggregate and water
    C. cement, sand, stone, and water
    D. gravel, cement, and water

14. If the blade of a screw driver is thicker than the slot at the top of a screw, the way to *properly* drive the screw into wood in this case is to

    A. widen the slot of the screw to fit the larger blade tip
    B. tap the end of the screw driver lightly to get a firmer hold into the screw slot
    C. get another screw driver which fits the size of the screw slot
    D. apply a drop of lubricating oil to the screw slot to get the screw started into the wood

QUESTIONS 15-20.
Questions 15 through 20 are to be answered *solely* on the basis of the following passage.

The basic hand-operated hoisting device is the tackle or purchase, consisting of a line called a fall, reeved through one or more blocks.

To hoist a load of given size, you must set up a rig with a safe working load equal to or in excess of the load to be hoisted. In order to do this, you must be able to calculate the safe working load of a single part of line of given size; the safe working load of a given purchase which contains a line of given size; and the minimum size of hooks or shackles which you must use in a given type of purchase to hoist a given load. You must also be able to calculate the thrust which a given load will exert on a gin pole or a set of shears inclined at a given angle; the safe working load which a spar of a given size, used as a gin pole or as one of a set of shears, will sustain; and the stress which a given load will set up in the back guy of a gin pole, or in the back guy of a set of shears, inclined at a given angle.

15. The above passage refers to the lifting of loads by means of

    A. erected scaffolds   B. manual rigging devices
    C. power-driven equipment   D. conveyor belts

16. It can be concluded from the above passage, that a set of shears serves to

    A. absorb the force and stress of the working load
    B. operate the tackle
    C. contain the working load
    D. compute the safe working load

17. According to the above passage, a spar can be used for a

    A. back guy   B. block   C. fall   D. gin pole

18. According to the above passage, the rule that a user of hand-operated tackle MUST follow is to make sure that the safe working load is at LEAST

    A. equal to the weight of the given load
    B. twice the combined weight of the block and falls
    C. one-half the weight of the given load
    D. twice the weight of the given load

19. According to the above passage, the two parts that make up a tackle are

    A. back guys and gin poles   B. blocksm and falls
    C. rigs and shears   D. spars and shackles

20. According to the above passage, in order to determine whether it is safe to hoist a particular load, you MUST   20._____

    A. use the maximum size hooks
    B. time the speed to bring a given load to a desired place
    C. calculate the forces exerted on various types of rigs
    D. repeatedly lift and lower various loads

KEY (CORRECT ANSWERS)

1.	C	11.	D
2.	C	12.	B
3.	C	13.	C
4.	A	14.	C
5.	C	15.	B
6.	B	16.	A
7.	C	17.	D
8.	B	18.	A
9.	B	19.	B
10.	C	20.	C

EXAMINATION SECTION
TEST 1

DIRECTIONS: Each question or incomplete statement is followed by several suggested answers or completions. Select the one that BEST answers the question or completes the statement. *PRINT THE LETTER OF THE CORRECT ANSWER IN THE SPACE AT THE RIGHT.*

1. The flow of oil in an automatic rotary cup oil burner is regulated by a(n) 1.____

   A. thermostat
   B. metering valve
   C. pressure relief valve
   D. electric eye

2. The type of fuel which must be *pre-heated* before it can be burned efficiently is 2.____

   A. natural gas
   B. pea coal
   C. Number 2 oil
   D. Number 6 oil

3. A suction gauge in a fuel-oil transfer system is *usually* located 3.____

   A. *before* the strainer
   B. *after* the strainer and *before* the pump
   C. *after* the pump and *before* the pressure relief valve
   D. *after* the pressure relief valve

4. The FIRST item that should be checked before starting the fire in a steam boiler is the 4.____

   A. thermostat
   B. vacuum pump
   C. boiler water level
   D. steam pressure

5. Operation of a boiler that has been *sealed* by the department of buildings is 5.____

   A. prohibited
   B. permitted when the outside temperature is below 32° F
   C. permitted between the hours of 6:00 A.M. and 8:00 A.M. and 9:00 P.M. and 11:00 P.M.
   D. permitted only for the purposes of heating domestic water

6. Lowering the thermostat setting by 5 degrees during the heating season will result in a fuel saving of, *most nearly*, _____ percent. 6.____

   A. 2   B. 5   C. 20   D. 50

7. An electrically-driven rotary fuel oil pump must be protected from internal damage by the installation in the oil line of a 7.____

   A. discharge-side strainer
   B. check valve
   C. suction gauge
   D. pressure relief valve

8. The air pollution code states that no person shall cause or permit the emission of an air contaminant of a density which appears as dark or darker than Number _____ on the standard smoke chart. 8.____

   A. One
   B. Two
   C. Three
   D. Four

9. When a glass globe is put back over a newly-replaced light bulb in a ceiling light fixture, the holding screws on the globe should be tightened, then loosened one half turn.
   This is done MAINLY to prevent

   A. fires caused by electrical short circuits
   B. cracking of the globe due to heat expansion
   C. falling of the globe from the light fixture
   D. building up of harmful gases inside the globe

10. Standard 120-volt plug-type fuses are *generally* rated in

   A. farads   B. ohms   C. watts   D. amperes

11. Standard 120-volt electric light bulbs are *generally* rated in

   A. farads   B. ohms   C. watts   D. amperes

12. A cleaner informs you that his electrical vacuum cleaner is not working even though he tried the off-on switch several times and checked to see that the plug was still in the wall outlet.
    Of the following, the FIRST course of action you should take in this situation is to

    A. determine if the circuit-breaker has tripped out
    B. take apart the vacuum cleaner
    C. replace the electric cord on the vacuum cleaner
    D. replace the electrical outlet

13. The one of the following that is the MOST practical method for a building custodian to use in making a temporary repair in a straight portion of a water pipe which has a small leak is to

    A. attach a clamped patch over the leak
    B. weld or braze the pipe, depending on the material
    C. drill and tap the pipe, then insert a plug
    D. fill the hole with an epoxy sealer

14. The PRIMARY function of the packing which is generally found in the stuffing box of a centrifugal pump is to

    A. compensate for misalignment of the pump shaft
    B. prevent leakage of the fluid
    C. control the discharge rate of the pump
    D. provide support for the pump shaft

15. A pipe coupling is a plumbing fitting that is *most commonly* used to join

    A. two pieces of threaded pipe of the same diameter
    B. a large diameter tubing to a smaller diameter threaded pipe
    C. two pieces of threaded pipe of different diameters
    D. a large diameter threaded pipe to a smaller diameter tubing

16. Of the following, the MOST important reason for replacing a worn washer in a dripping faucet as soon as possible is to prevent

    A. overflow of the sink tap
    B. the mixture of hot and cold water in the sink
    C. damage to the faucet parts that can be the result of overtightening the stem
    D. air from entering the supply line

17. Window glass is secured mechanically in wood windows by

    A. glazing points B. enamel paint
    C. screws D. putty

18. In carpentry work, the *most commonly* used hand saw is the _____ saw.

    A. hack B. rip C. buck D. cross-cut

19. The device which *usually* keeps a doorknob from rotating on the spindle is a

    A. cotter pin B. tapered key
    C. set screw D. stop screw

20. The *one* of the following types of nails that *usually* requires the use of a tool known as a nail set is the _____ nail.

    A. finishing B. sheet rock C. 6-penny D. cut

21. The following tasks are frequently done when an office is cleaned:
    I. The floor is vacuumed.
    II. The ash trays and waste baskets are emptied.
    III. The desks and furniture are dusted.
    The ORDER in which these tasks should *generally* be done is:

    A. I, II, III B. II, III, I C. III, II, I D. I, III, II

22. When wax is applied to a floor by the use of a twine mop with handle, the wax should be _____ with the mop.

    A. applied in thin coats
    B. applied in heavy coats
    C. poured on the floor, then spread
    D. dropped on the floor, then spread

23. The BEST way to clean dust from an accoustical-type ceiling is with a

    A. strong soap solution B. wet sponge
    C. vacuum cleaner D. stream of water

24. Of the following, the MOST important reason why a wet mop should NOT be wrung out by hand is that

    A. the strings of the mop will be damaged by hand-wringing
    B. sharp objects picked up by the mop may injure the hands
    C. the mop cannot be made dry enough by hand-wringing
    D. fine dirt will become embedded in the strings of the mop

25. When a painted wall is washed by hand, the wall should be washed from the

   A. *top down,* with a soaking *wet* sponge
   B. *bottom up,* with a soaking *wet* sponge
   C. *top down,* with a *damp* sponge
   D. *bottom up,* with a *damp* sponge

26. When a painted wall is brushed with a clean lamb's wool duster, the duster should be drawn _____ with a _____ pressure.

   A. *downward; light*
   B. *upward; light*
   C. *downward; firm*
   D. *upward; firm*

27. The *one* of the following terms which BEST describes the size of a floor brush is

   A. 72-cubic inch
   B. 32-ounce
   C. 24-inch
   D. 10-square foot

28. Terrazzo floors should be mopped periodically with a(n)

   A. acid solution
   B. neutral detergent in warm water
   C. mop treated with kerosene
   D. strong alkaline solution

29. The MAIN reason why the handle of a reversible floor brush should be shifted from one side of the brush block to the opposite side is to

   A. change the angle at which the brush sweeps the floor
   B. give equal wear to both sides of the brush
   C. permit the brush to sweep hard-to-reach areas
   D. make it easier to sweep backward

30. When a long corridor is swept with a floor brush, it is *good* practice to

   A. push the brush with moderately long strokes and flick it after each stroke
   B. press on the brush and push it the whole length of the corridor in one sweep
   C. pull the brush inward with short, brisk strokes
   D. sweep across rather than down the length of the corridor

KEY (CORRECT ANSWERS)

1.	B	16.	C
2.	D	17.	A
3.	B	18.	D
4.	C	19.	C
5.	A	20.	A
6.	C	21.	B
7.	D	22.	A
8.	B	23.	C
9.	B	24.	B
10.	D	25.	D
11.	C	26.	A
12.	A	27.	C
13.	A	28.	B
14.	B	29.	B
15.	A	30.	A

TEST 2

DIRECTIONS: Each question or incomplete statement is followed by several suggested answers or completions. Select the one that BEST answers the question or completes the statement. *PRINT THE LETTER OF THE CORRECT ANSWER IN THE SPACE AT THE RIGHT.*

1. Of the following office cleaning jobs performed during the year, the *one* which should be done MOST frequently is

   A. cleaning the fluorescent lights
   B. dusting the Venetian blinds
   C. cleaning the bookcase glass
   D. carpet-sweeping the rug

2. The BEST polishing agent to use on wood furniture is

   A. pumice
   B. paste wax
   C. water emulsion wax
   D. neat's-foot oil

3. Lemon oil polish is used BEST to polish

   A. exterior bronze
   B. marble walls
   C. leather seats
   D. lacquered metal

4. Cleaning with trisodium phosphate is *most likely* to damage

   A. toilet bowls
   B. drain pipes
   C. polished marble floors
   D. rubber tile floors

5. Of the following cleaning agents, the one which should NOT be used to remove stains from urinals is

   A. caustic lye
   B. detergent
   C. oxalic acid
   D. muriatic acid

6. The one of the following cleaners which *generally* contains an abrasive is

   A. caustic lye
   B. trisodium phosphate
   C. scouring powder
   D. ammonia

7. The instructions on a box of cleaning powder say: *Mix one pound of cleaning powder in four gallons of water.* According to these instructions, how many ounces of cleaning powder should be mixed in one gallon of water?

   A. 4   B. 8   C. 12   D. 16

8. In accordance with recommended practice, a dust mop, when not being used, should be stored

   A. *hanging*, handle end down
   B. *hanging*, handle end up
   C. *standing* on the floor, handle end down
   D. *standing* on the floor, handle end up

2 (#2)

9. The two types of floors found in public buildings are classified as *hard floors* and *soft floors*.
An example of a *hard floor* is one made of

   A. linoleum
   B. cork
   C. ceramic tile
   D. asphalt tile

9.____

10. A squeegee is a tool that is MAINLY used to clean

   A. painted walls
   B. radiator covers
   C. window glass
   D. ceramic tile floors

10.____

11. The BEST way for a building custodian to determine whether a cleaner is doing his work well is by

   A. observing the cleaner at work for several hours
   B. asking the cleaner questions about the work
   C. asking other cleaners to rate his work
   D. inspecting the cleanliness of the spaces assigned to the cleaner

11.____

12. The PRIMARY purpose of using a disinfectant material is to

   A. kill germs
   B. destroy odors
   C. remove stains
   D. kill insects

12.____

13. Windows should be washed by using a solution of warm water mixed with

   A. chlorine bleach
   B. kerosene
   C. ammonia
   D. soft soap

13.____

14. Of the following, the MOST effective way to reduce waste of cleaning tools is to

   A. keep careful records of how often tools are issued
   B. require that the old tool be returned before issuing a new one
   C. require that all tools be used for a fixed number of hours before replacing them
   D. train the cleaners to use the tools properly

14.____

15. The number of square feet of unobstructed corridor floor space that a cleaner should sweep in an hour is, *most nearly*,

   A. 1200   B. 2400   C. 4000   D. 6000

15.____

16. Sweeping compound is used on concrete floors MAINLY to

   A. polish the floor
   B. keep the dust down
   C. soften the encrusted dirt
   D. provide a non-slip surface

16.____

17. The BEST attachment to use on an electric scrubbing machine when stripping waxed resilient flooring is a

   A. nylon disk
   B. soft brush
   C. steel wool pad
   D. pumice wheel

17.____

57

18. A counter brush is BEST suited to cleaning

    A. water cooler drains B. radiators
    C. light fixtures D. lavatory fixtures

19. Improper use of a carbon-dioxide type portable fire extinguisher may cause injury to the operator because

    A. handling the nozzle during discharge can cause frostbite to the skin
    B. carbon dioxide is highly poisonous if breathed into the lungs
    C. use of carbon dioxide on an oil fire can cause a chemical explosion
    D. the powdery residue left by the discharge is highly caustic to the skin

20. When using a portable single ladder with ten rungs, the GREATEST number of rungs that a cleaner should climb up is

    A. 7 B. 8 C. 9 D. 10

21. Of the following types of portable fire extinguishers, the one which should be used to control a fire in or around live electrical equipment is the _____ type.

    A. foam B. soda-acid
    C. carbon-dioxide D. gas-cartridge water

22. The MOST frequent cause of accidental injuries to workers on the job is

    A. unsafe working practices of employees
    B. poor design of buildings and working areas
    C. lack of warning signs in hazardous working areas
    D. lack of adequate safety guards on equipment and machinery

23. Of the following, the MOST important purpose of preparing an accident report on an injury to a cleaner is to help

    A. collect statistics on different types of accidents
    B. calm the feelings of the injured cleaner
    C. prevent similar accidents in the future
    D. prove that the cleaner was at fault

24. The one of the following types of locks that is used on emergency exit doors is the _____ bolt.

    A. panic B. dead C. cinch D. toggle

25. The one of the following types of locks that *usually* contains both a live bolt and a dead bolt is a _____ lock.

    A. mortise B. double-hung window
    C. loose pin butt D. window frame

KEY (CORRECT ANSWERS)

1. D
2. B
3. A
4. C
5. D

6. C
7. A
8. B
9. C
10. C

11. D
12. A
13. C
14. D
15. D

16. B
17. A
18. B
19. A
20. B

21. C
22. A
23. C
24. A
25. A

———

EXAMINATION SECTION
TEST 1

DIRECTIONS: Each question or incomplete statement is followed by several suggested answers or completions. Select the one that BEST answers the question or completes the statement. *PRINT THE LETTER OF THE CORRECT ANSWER IN THE SPACE AT THE RIGHT.*

1. Before starting any lawn mowing, the distance between the blade and a flat surface should be measured with a ruler.
 The distance should be such that the cut of the grass above the ground is _____ inch(es).
 A. 1 B. 1½ C. 2 D. 3

 1._____

2. Strainers in a number 6 fuel oil system should be checked once a
 A. day B. week C. month D. year

 2._____

3. The spinning cup on a rotary cup oil burner should be cleaned
 A. once a day
 B. once a week
 C. every 2 weeks
 D. once a month

 3._____

4. Terrazzo floors should be cleaned daily with a
 A. damp mop using clear water
 B. damp mop using a strong alkaline solution
 C. damp mop treated with vegetable oil

 4._____

5. New installations of vinyl-asbestos floor should
 A. never be machine scrubbed
 B. be dry buffed weekly
 C. be swept daily, using an oily compound
 D. never be swept with treated dust mops

 5._____

6. Standpipe fire hose shall be inspected
 A. monthly
 B. quarterly
 C. semi-annually
 D. annually

 6._____

7. All portable fire extinguishers shall be inspected once
 A. a year
 B. a month
 C. a week
 D. every 3 months

 7._____

8. Soda-acid and foam-type fire extinguishers shall be discharged and recharged AT LEAST once
 A. each year
 B. every 2 years
 C. every 6 months
 D. each month

 8._____

9. Elevator *safeties* under the car shall be tested once each
   A. day B. week C. month D. quarter

10. Key-type fire alarms in public school buildings shall be tested
    A. daily B. weekly C. monthly D. quarterly

11. Combustion efficiency can be determined from an appropriate chart used in conjunction with
    A. steam temperature and steam pressure
    B. flue gas temperature and percentage of CO_2
    C. flue gas temperature and fuel heating value
    D. oil temperature and steam pressure

12. In the combustion of common fuels, the MAJOR boiler heat loss is due to
    A. incomplete combustion
    B. moisture in the fuel
    C. heat radiation
    D. heat lost in the flue gases

13. The MOST important reason for blowing down a boiler water column and gauge glass is to
    A. prevent the gauge glass level from rising too high
    B. relieve stresses in the gauge glass
    C. insure a true water level reading
    D. insure a true pressure gauge reading

14. The secondary voltage of a transformer used for ignition in a fuel oil burner has a range of MOST NEARLY _____ volts to _____ volts.
    A. 120; 240 B. 440; 660 C. 660; 1,200 D. 5,000; 15,000

15. Assume that during the month of April there were 3 days with an average outdoor temperature of 30°F, 7 days with 40°F, 10 days with 50°F, 3 days with 60°F, and 7 days with 65°F.
    The number of degree days for the month was
    A. 330 B. 445 C. 595 D. 1,150

16. The pH of boiler feedwater is USUALLY maintained within the range of
    A. 4 to 5 B. 6 to 7 C. 10 to 12 D. 13 to 14

17. The admission of steam to the coils of a domestic hot water supply tank is regulated by a(n)
    A. pressure regulating valve
    B. immersion type temperature gauge
    C. check valve
    D. thermostatic control valve

18. The device which senses primary air failure in a rotary cup oil burner is USUALLY called a(n)
    A. vaporstate
    B. anemometer
    C. venture
    D. pressure gauge

3 (#1)

19. The device which starts and stops the flow of oil into an automatic rotary cup oil burner is USUALLY called a(n) _____ valve.
    A. magnetic oil   B. oil metering   C. oil check   D. relief

19.____

20. A vacuum breaker used on a steam-heated domestic hot water tank is USUALLY connected to the
    A. circulating pump
    B. tank wall
    C. aquastat
    D. steam coil flange

20.____

21. A vacuum pump in a low pressure steam heating system which is equipped with a float switch, a vacuum switch, a magnetic starter, and a selector switch, can be operated on
    A. float, vacuum, or automatic
    B. float, vacuum, or continuous
    C. vacuum, automatic, or continuous
    D. float, automatic, or continuous

21.____

22. If the temperature of the condensate returning to the vacuum pump in a low pressure steam vacuum heating system is above 180°F, the trouble may be caused by
    A. faulty radiator traps
    B. room thermostats being set too high
    C. uninsulated return lines
    D. too many radiators being shut off

22.____

23. A feedwater regulator operates to
    A. shut down the burner when the water is low
    B. maintain the water in the boiler at a predetermined level
    C. drain the water in the boiler
    D. regulate the temperature of the feedwater

23.____

24. An automatically fired steam boiler is equipped with an automatic low water cut-off.
    The low water cut-off is USUALLY actuated by
    A. steam pressure
    B. fuel pressure
    C. float action
    D. water temperature

24.____

25. Low pressure steam or an electric heater is USUALLY required for heating _____ fuel.
    A. #1   B. #2   C. #4   D. #6

25.____

KEY (CORRECT ANSWERS)

1.	C	11.	B
2.	A	12.	D
3.	A	13.	C
4.	A	14.	D
5.	B	15.	B
6.	B	16.	C
7.	B	17.	D
8.	A	18.	A
9.	C	19.	A
10.	A	20.	D

21. D
22. A
23. B
24. C
25. D

TEST 2

DIRECTIONS: Each question or incomplete statement is followed by several suggested answers or completions. Select the one that BEST answers the question or completes the statement. *PRINT THE LETTER OF THE CORRECT ANSWER IN THE SPACE AT THE RIGHT.*

1. A compound gauge is calibrated to read
   A. pressure only
   B. vacuum only
   C. vacuum and pressure
   D. temperature and humidity

2. In a mechanical pressure-atomizing type oil burner, the oil is automized by using an automizing tip and
   A. steam pressure
   B. pump pressure
   C. compressed air
   D. a spinning cup

3. A good over-the-fire draft in a natural draft furnace should be APPROXIMATELY _____ inch(es) of water _____.
   A. 5.0; positive pressure
   B. 0.05; positive pressure
   C. 0.05; vacuum
   D. 5.0; vacuum

4. When it is necessary to add chemicals to a heating boiler, it should be done
   A. immediately after boiler blowdown
   B. after the boiler has been cleaned internally of sludge, scale, and other foreign matter
   C. at periods when condensate flow to the boiler is small
   D. at a time when there is a heavy flow of condensate to the boiler

5. The modutrol motor on a rotary cup oil burner burning #6 fuel oil automatically operates the primary air damper,
   A. secondary air damper, and oil metering valve
   B. secondary air damper, and magnetic oil valve
   C. oil metering valve, and magnetic oil valve
   D. and magnetic oil valve

6. The manual-reset pressuretrol is classified as a _____ Control.
   A. Safety and Operating
   B. Limit and Operating
   C. Limit and Safety
   D. Limit, Operating, and Safety

7. Sodium sulphite is added to boiler feedwater to
   A. avoid caustic embrittlement
   B. increase the pH value
   C. reduce the tendency of foaming in the steam drum
   D. remove dissolved oxygen

8. Neat cement is a mixture of cement,
   A. putty, and water
   B. and water
   C. lime, and water
   D. salt, and water

9. In a concrete mix of 1:2:4, the 2 refers to the amount of
   A. sand   B. cement   C. stone   D. water

10. The word *natatorium* means MOST NEARLY a(n)
    A. auditorium
    B. playroom
    C. gymnasium
    D. indoor swimming pool

11. Plated metal surfaces which are protected by a thin coat of clear lacquer should be cleaned with a(n)
    A. abrasive compound
    B. liquid polish
    C. mild soap solution
    D. lemon oil solution

12. Wet mop filler replacements are ordered by
    A. length
    B. weight
    C. number of strands
    D. trade number

13. The BEST way to determine the value of a cleaning material is by
    A. performance testing
    B. manufacturer's literature
    C. written specifications
    D. interviews with manufacturer's salesman

14. Instructions on a container of cleaning compound state: *Mix one pound of compound in 5 gallons of water.*
    Using these instructions, the amount of compound which should be added to 15 quarts of water is MOST NEARLY _____ ounces.
    A. 3   B. 8   C. 12   D. 48

15. The MOST usual cause of paint blisters is
    A. too much oil in the paint
    B. moisture under the paint coat
    C. a heavy coat of paint
    D. improper drying of paint

16. The floor that should NOT be machine scrubbed is a(n)
    A. lobby
    B. lunchroom
    C. gymnasium
    D. auditorium aisle

17. Pick-up sweeping in a public building is the occasional removal of the more conspicuous loose dirt from corridors and lobbies.
    This type of sweeping should be done
    A. after scrubbing or waving of floors
    B. with the aid of a sweeping compound
    C. at night after school hours
    D. during regular school hours

18. According to recommended practice, when a steam boiler is taken out of service for a long period of time, the boiler drum should FIRST be
    A. drained completely while the water is hot (above 212°F)
    B. drained completely after the water has been cooled down to 180°F
    C. filled completely without draining
    D. filled to the level of the top try cock

18.____

19. The prevention and control of vermin and rodents in a building is PRIMARILY a matter of
    A. maintaining good housekeeping on a continuous basis
    B. periodic use of an exterminator's service
    C. calling in the exterminator when necessary
    D. cleaning the building thoroughly during school vacation

19.____

20. If it is not possible to plant new shrubs immediately upon delivery in the spring, they should be stored in a(n)
    A. sheltered outdoor area   B. unsheltered outdoor area
    C. boiler room   D. warm place indoors

20.____

21. Peat moss is generally used for its
    A. food value   B. nitrogen
    C. alkalinity   D. moisture retaining quality

21.____

22. The legal minimum age of employees engaged for cleaning windows in the state is _____ years.
    A. 16   B. 17   C. 18   D. 21

22.____

23. The MAIN classification of lumber used for construction purposes is known as _____ lumber.
    A. industrial   B. commercial   C. finish   D. yard

23.____

24. Specifications concerning window cleaners' anchors and safety belts must be in compliance with the rules and regulations outlined in the
    A. state labor law and board of standards and appeals
    B. city building code
    C. fire department safety manual
    D. national protection code

24.____

25. Pruning of street trees is the responsibility of the
    A. custodian-engineer   B. board of education
    C. department of parks   D. borough president's office

25.____

KEY (CORRECT ANSWERS)

1.	C		11.	C
2.	B		12.	B
3.	C		13.	A
4.	D		14.	C
5.	A		15.	B
6.	C		16.	C
7.	D		17.	D
8.	B		18.	B
9.	A		19.	A
10.	D		20.	A

21. D
22. C
23. D
24. A
25. C

EXAMINATION SECTION
TEST 1

DIRECTIONS: Each question or incomplete statement is followed by several suggested answers or completions. Select the one that BEST answers the question or completes the statement. *PRINT THE LETTER OF THE CORRECT ANSWER IN THE SPACE AT THE RIGHT.*

1. Which of the following substances causes asphalt tile to turn spongy? 1._____

    A. Oil   B. Varnish   C. Water   D. Dust

2. Which of the following would NOT cause asphalt tile to turn yellow? 2._____

    A. A layer of dust   B. Varnish
    C. Lacquer   D. Water

3. Which one of the following is LEAST likely to be an advantage of waxing a floor? 3._____

    A. Helps to make a room quieter
    B. Helps to reduce wear on the floor
    C. Gives a pleasant shine to the floor
    D. Improves the stain resistance of the floor

4. The action of liquid cleaner on a floor with built-up wax is to 4._____

    A. make the wax disappear into the air
    B. turn the wax into little grains that must be swept up in a vacuum cleaner
    C. soften the wax, which has to be scrubbed away and then rinsed off
    D. make the floor waterproof

5. After how many waxings should built-up wax be removed from a floor? Every 5._____

    A. waxing   B. 3 waxings
    C. 6 waxings   D. 12 waxings

6. Manuals on floor cleaning describe methods of cleaning *resilient flooring.* Which of the following kinds of flooring surfaces is NOT *resilient*? _____ tile. 6._____

    A. Cork   B. Asphalt   C. Vinyl   D. Terrazzo

7. In buffing a floor, it is NOT desirable to use a polishing brush because the 7._____

    A. brush will scratch the surface you are trying to polish
    B. strands of the brush fall out easily
    C. brush is often used for other purposes
    D. brush does not usually remove deep scuff marks

8. *Rolling* results when only the upper parts of a wax coat dry, leaving the lower parts wet. In waxing a floor, this condition comes from 8._____

    A. putting on too thick a coat of wax
    B. putting on too thin a coat of wax

C. rinsing the floor before applying the wax
D. leaving soap on the floor before applying the wax

9. After a cork or linoleum floor is installed, how long should you wait before you mop the floor for the FIRST time?

   A. 1 day   B. 3 days   C. 12 hours   D. 2 weeks

10. On sweeping stairways, you should direct your men to make a practice of sweeping them

    A. when tenant traffic is heavy, so that people can see them working
    B. whenever they have free time during the day
    C. during the morning at a time when tenant traffic is lightest
    D. in the middle of the day, when the traffic is medium heavy

11. How often must public corridors be swept?

    A. Only when a visible amount of dirt piles up
    B. Every day
    C. Once a week
    D. Every three days

12. You should NOT use an oily mop to sweep any floor because it

    A. leaves a sticky film that can catch dust
    B. eats away at the floor like acid
    C. makes the floor completely waterproof
    D. prevents wax from being applied

13. Which of the following would NOT be used on a concrete floor?

    A. Water base wax   B. Oily sweeping compound
    C. Solvent wax   D. Wire brush

14. You should NOT use an alkaline cleaner on linoleum floors because the cleaner

    A. will make the floor shine too brightly
    B. makes the linoleum sticky
    C. makes the linoleum crack and curl
    D. costs too much to be practical

15. The BEST way of wet mopping a large floor area is to mop the floor area

    A. with a circular motion
    B. from side to side or with a figure 8 motion
    C. with forward and back strokes
    D. alternate side to side and forward and back

16. The type of product to use when cleaning terrazzo floors is

    A. mild cleaner   B. diluted acid solution
    C. scouring powder   D. paste wax

17. A caretaker was met mopping an asphalt tile floor. He decided to make the floor as wet as possible.
    For him to do this is a

    A. *good* idea, because the more water you use, the cleaner the floor will be
    B. *bad* idea, because water should never be wasted
    C. *good* idea, because the floor will not have to be washed as often
    D. *bad* idea, because the excess water will eventually damage the floor surface

    17.____

18. When you wet clean a stairway by hand, you need two buckets.
    One of them is for the cleaning solution, and the other one is used for

    A. extra ammonia for cleaning
    B. rinsing, and should be filled with clean water
    C. putting out fires, and should be filled with sand
    D. storage of equipment

    18.____

19. The cleaning of stairways is USUALLY scheduled to be done with

    A. corridor cleaning
    B. sidewalk cleaning
    C. incinerator work
    D. move-outs

    19.____

20. *Dry cleaning* in relation to a building refers to

    A. a reconditioning process that restores the appearance of a floor and protects the surface by buffing
    B. dusting of a wall area with specially treated cloth in order to produce a sheen
    C. patch waxing of a floor with a powdered wax compound
    D. dry mopping only of a floor area

    20.____

Questions 21-25.

DIRECTIONS: Questions 21 through 25 are to be answered ONLY according to the information given in the following paragraph.

In order to help prevent the spread of fire, it is necessary to understand the means by which heat is transmitted. Heat is transmitted through solids by a method called *conduction*. Materials vary greatly in their ability to transmit heat. Metals are good conductors of heat. On the other hand, wood, glass, pottery, asbestos, and many like substances are very poor conductors of heat and are termed insulators. It should be remembered, however, that there are no perfect insulators of heat. All will conduct heat to some extent, and if the heat continues long enough, it will be transmitted through the solid. The hazard of heat transmission is illustrated by the fact that a fire on one side of a metal wall could start a fire on the other side if combustibles were close to the wall.

21. Of the following, the BEST material to use for the handle of a metal pan to guard against heat is

    A. copper   B. iron   C. wood   D. steel

    21.____

22. According to the above paragraph, *conduction* applies to the traveling of heat through a

    A. solid
    B. liquid
    C. slow-moving fluid
    D. gas

    22.____

23. According to the information in the above paragraph, when storing combustible materials in a room with metal walls, it is BEST to   23.___

    A. keep the combustibles close together
    B. keep the combustibles away from the metal walls
    C. put the non-metals nearest the metal walls
    D. separate metal materials from non-metal materials

24. Based on the information in the above paragraph, which one of the following objects is the BEST conductor of heat?   24.___

    A. Pottery   B. An oak desk
    C. A glass jar   D. A silver spoon

25. Of the following, the title which BEST describes what the above paragraph is about is   25.___

    A. Uses of Conductors and Insulators
    B. The Reasons Why Fire Spreads
    C. Heat Transmission and Fires
    D. The Hazards of Poor Conduction

KEY (CORRECT ANSWERS)

1.	A	11.	B
2.	A	12.	A
3.	A	13.	B
4.	C	14.	C
5.	C	15.	B
6.	D	16.	A
7.	D	17.	D
8.	A	18.	B
9.	B	19.	A
10.	C	20.	A

21. C
22. A
23. B
24. D
25. C

TEST 2

DIRECTIONS: Each question or incomplete statement is followed by several suggested answers or completions. Select the one that BEST answers the question or completes the statement. *PRINT THE LETTER OF THE CORRECT ANSWER IN THE SPACE AT THE RIGHT.*

1. If it is necessary to wash stairways, this should be done during the

    A. day
    B. night
    C. weekend
    D. morning rush hour

    1._____

2. A caretaker noticed that a family was moving out. He gave the following information to the foreman: name and apartment number of the family and the van license number. Which one of the following facts did the caretaker leave out that he should have given to the foreman?

    A. Registration number of the moving van
    B. Inspection date of the moving van
    C. Name of the moving company
    D. Names and addresses of the movers

    2._____

3. A caretaker sees that a lock on the outside door of a project building has been broken by vandals.
   This should be reported FIRST to the

    A. housing manager
    B. foreman of caretakers
    C. building superintendent
    D. assistant building superintendent

    3._____

4. In housing authority practice, a garage broom is *usually* used to sweep

    A. small asphalt walks
    B. playgrounds
    C. small cement walks
    D. incinerator rooms

    4._____

5. Listed below, and numbered in scrambled order, are the first four steps to follow when you are dusting furniture:
    I. Move objects on furniture and dust under them
    II. Refold cloth
    III. Dust furniture itself
    IV. Fold the dusting cloth

    The CORRECT order of these steps should be:

    A. I, IV, III, II
    B. III, IV, II, I
    C. IV, II, I, III
    D. IV, III, II, I

    5._____

6. Snow removal should begin

    A. after the snow has been packed solid
    B. as soon as possible
    C. when the depth is more than 2 inches
    D. when the weather bureau says it is a *heavy snowfall*

    6._____

7. On which of the following should you advise a caretaker to use a corn broom?

   A. Basement areas B. Stair halls
   C. Rubber tile floor D. Window sills

8. Chrome fixtures should be cleaned by

   A. using a mild soap solution then polishing with a soft cloth
   B. dusting lightly, then wax with oil base wax
   C. polishing with a scouring pad
   D. washing with a solution of water and ammonia, then rinsing with a detergent

9. The MAIN reason caretakers are advised to wear protective goggles while changing a broken bulb is to avoid the danger of

   A. glare from the bulb
   B. pieces of glass getting in the eyes
   C. sparks from the bulb
   D. insects on or around the bulb socket

10. Oily rags should be placed in a container made of

    A. metal B. cardboard
    C. cloth D. wood

11. When a caretaker lights an incinerator in the morning, the door to the incinerator room should be

    A. all the way open
    B. all the way closed
    C. half-way open, to let the air in
    D. open or closed, depending on the weather

12. Wood and cork floors should be sealed because

    A. these surfaces have tiny natural openings that can trap dirt and grease
    B. it keeps these kinds of floors from warping and buckling
    C. it makes the surface stronger
    D. the sealing process makes the surface easier to walk on

13. A single 8-foot ladder is to be used for a certain window washing job.
    Of the distances from the wall which are given below, which one is BEST to place the ladder from the wall? _____ feet.

    A. 2 B. 4 C. 6 D. 8

14. To lift something without injury to yourself, you should obey all of the following rules EXCEPT:

    A. Keep your back straight
    B. Get help with heavy loads
    C. Lift quickly with your arms
    D. Stand close to what you are lifting

3 (#2)

15. The type of product to use when cleaning asphalt tile is 15.____

    A. sandpaper pad B. plain ammonia
    C. water base wax D. oil base polish

16. When you are taking a mop outfit with wringer through a corridor, it is VERY important to proceed slowly past doorways because 16.____

    A. you might slip and hurt yourself
    B. you should look for any cracks in the floor
    C. you must watch out for people who might come through the doorway
    D. the doorway area is more slippery than the rest of the corridor

17. Which one of the following is the MOST important piece of clothing to wear while cleaning an incinerator? 17.____

    A. Leather boots B. Fireman's helmet
    C. Heavy coat D. Work gloves

18. Of the following, who should hang the elevator pads to be used when tenants move in or out? 18.____
    The

    A. foreman of housing caretakers
    B. tenant himself
    C. caretaker assigned to the building
    D. elevator mechanic

19. One day a caretaker said to his foreman, *I can get a tile cleaner that is as good as the stuff we use, and for less money, because my brother is a building contractor. How about it?* 19.____
    The CORRECT way for the foreman to handle this situation is for him to

    A. thank the caretaker, but tell him that individual caretakers cannot buy their own cleaning material for project use
    B. tell the caretaker that no one has any right to start interfering in the buying procedures of the housing authority
    C. go along with the caretaker and buy the cleaner from his brother, because it might save money for the authority
    D. tell the caretaker to have his brother contact the project manager

20. A new caretaker under your supervision is waxing a floor for the first time. While the job seems to be going along well, he is not doing it quite the way you asked him to do it and so is taking longer than he should. 20.____
    Which of the following is the BEST action for you to take under these conditions?

    A. Leave him to finish the job and go on to the next one
    B. Interrupt him and tell him to do the job the way he was taught
    C. Tell him he is doing well but that he should do better
    D. Explain to him why your way is faster and tell him to try it

21. The EASIEST way to find out how many supplies you have available is for you to 21.____

    A. look at last year's figures
    B. keep an up-to-date inventory

C. ask one of your men to let you know
D. check the availability when you use a special item

Questions 22-23.

DIRECTIONS: Questions 22 and 23 are to be answered on the basis of information in the following paragraph.

Studies show that the average high-class office building has a tenant population of around 750 persons per 100,000 square feet of area and that the elevators normally have to handle from seven to ten times as many passengers per day as the total number of permanent occupants.

22. Based on the above, what would be the AVERAGE tenant population of a building having 300,000 square feet of space?

    A. 1,000 B. 2,250 C. 2,200 D. 750

23. Based on the above, how many passengers would the elevator have to handle per day if the area of the building is 100,000 square feet?
    From

    A. 5,250 to 7,500 B. 750 to 1,500
    C. 1,000 to 2,500 D. 2,500 to 5,000

Questions 24-25.

DIRECTIONS: Questions 24 and 25 are to be answered on the basis of information in the paragraph below.

A large number of studies show that in diversified tenancy buildings, the maximum five-minute morning incoming traffic flow averages 12% of the building population and that the noon peak at its highest five-minute period averages about 15% of the building, population.

24. Based on the above, with a building population of 1,000, how many people would the elevators have to handle during the MAXIMUM incoming morning traffic period?

    A. 120 B. 130 C. 150 D. 160

25. How many people during the highest five-minute peak period of the noon rush hour would the elevator be able to handle at MAXIMUM capacity with a building population of 1,000?

    A. 120 B. 125 C. 150 D. 175

KEY (CORRECT ANSWERS)

1. C
2. C
3. B
4. B
5. D

6. B
7. A
8. A
9. B
10. A

11. B
12. A
13. A
14. C
15. C

16. C
17. D
18. C
19. A
20. D

21. B
22. B
23. A
24. A
25. C

EXAMINATION SECTION

TEST 1

DIRECTIONS: Each question or incomplete statement is followed by several suggested answers or completions. Select the one that BEST answers the question or completes the statement. *PRINT THE LETTER OF THE CORRECT ANSWER IN THE SPACE AT THE RIGHT.*

1. An unusually high vacuum reading in a fuel oil suction line may indicate that the
    A. level in the fuel oil tank is low
    B. oil preheater is leaking
    C. oil strainer is dirty
    D. oil is too hot

    1._____

2. The MAIN reason for modulating the flame in a steam heating boiler that has an automatic rotary cup oil burner is to
    A. reduce the number of start and stop operations
    B. guarantee a high-fire start
    C. vary the cut-out pressure
    D. vary the cut-in pressure

    2._____

3. The device on a rotary cup oil burner which senses primary air failure is the
    A. draft sensing device
    B. aquastat
    C. draft alarm
    D. vaporstat

    3._____

4. A 10,000-gallon pressurized house tank contains 8,030 gallons of water, and the pressure gauge reads 60 psi. In the event of a power failure, the number of gallons of water which can be drawn out of the tank before the pressure reading drops to 50 psi is MOST NEARLY
    A. 300 B. 2,000 C. 6,000 D. 8,000

    4._____

5. The heat balancer in a Dunham steam heating system
    A. measures indoor temperatures
    B. controls the firing rate of two or more boilers
    C. measures outdoor temperatures
    D. reacts to the rate of heat output

    5._____

6. In a sub-atmospheric steam heating system, the steam temperature corresponding to a vacuum of 15 inches of mercury is MOST NEARLY _____ °F.
    A. 180 B. 200 C. 212 D. 218

    6._____

7. When the fuel supply to a rotary cup oil burner is cut off, the burner motor switch should open within _____ seconds.
    A. 2 B. 4 to 8 C. 12 to 18 D. 30 to 40

    7._____

8. The proper method of laying up a steam boiler, for a period of less than one month, is to
    A. drain all the water and let the boiler dry out
    B. fill it with treated water to the top of the tubes
    C. fill it with treated water to the stop valve
    D. fill it with treated water to the level of the upper try cock

9. In the winter time, heating complaints by tenants should be investigated
    A. only if there are several complaints from one building
    B. only if the outside temperature is below 40°F
    C. immediately
    D. by the assistant superintendent

10. Compared to the input of an electric ignition transformer associated with #6 oil burners, the output is _____ voltage, _____ current.
    A. higher; higher
    B. higher; lower
    C. lower; higher
    D. lower; lower

11. A pressure regulator valve in a compressed air line should be
    A. preceded by a water and oil separator
    B. preceded by a solenoid valve
    C. followed by a water and oil separator
    D. followed by a solenoid valve

12. A preventive maintenance program in a boiler room should provide for the routine periodic replacement of
    A. badly leaking boiler tubes
    B. electric motors
    C. safety valve springs
    D. programmer electronic tubes

13. Steam-heated hot water tank coils can be tested for leaks by
    A. chemically testing the domestic hot water leaving the tank
    B. chemically testing the condensate leaving the coil
    C. pressure testing the domestic water in the tank
    D. pressure testing the condensate return

14. The chemical which is added to boiler water to reduce its oxygen content is sodium
    A. carbonate
    B. chloride
    C. alginate
    D. sulphite

15. Wear in the sleeve bearings of an electric motor is MOST likely to result in a change in the
    A. pole spacing
    B. armature balance
    C. air gap
    D. line frequency

16. *Found reading* and *left reading* are terms associated with
    A. petrometers
    B. electric meters
    C. gas meters
    D. water meters

17. The FIRST priority in snow removal in a housing project is to remove snow from the
    A. building entrance steps and entrance landings
    B. perimeter sidewalks
    C. access to fuel oil fill lines and fire hydrants
    D. interior sidewalks leading from buildings to perimeter sidewalks

18. On Memorial Day, the National Flag should be flown at
    A. full staff all day
    B. half staff in the morning and full staff from noon to sunset
    C. half staff all day
    D. full staff in the morning and at half staff from noon to sunset

19. The common name for a tree called Quercus Alba is
    A. pine
    B. maple
    C. oak
    D. cedar

20. A tree which is considered to be suitable for street curb planting should
    A. grow rapidly
    B. have colorful foliage
    C. be an evergreen
    D. be straight and symmetrical

21. A roofing bond is
    A. the material used to cement the roofing layers to each other
    B. a guarantee by the manufacturer of the roofing material
    C. a guarantee by the contractor who installed the roof
    D. a vapor barrier

22. Window shade cloth has a calculated service life of _____ years.
    A. 2   B. 4   C. 6   D. 8

23. A resin-base floor finish USUALLY
    A. gives the highest luster of all floor finishes
    B. cannot be used on asphalt tile
    C. must be applied in heavy coats
    D. provides an anti-slip surface

24. The cause of paint blisters on wood is USUALLY
    A. moisture under the paint coat
    B. too thick a coat of paint
    C. too much oil in the paint
    D. plaster pores not sealed properly

25. When waxing asphalt tile floors, the wax should be applied in several thin coats because
    A. one thick coat takes longer to apply
    B. it will dry faster and harder
    C. it is a more economical method
    D. the pores of the tile will be able to absorb the wax more readily

26. A supplier quotes a list price of $14.00 for a replacement part less discounts of 25, 10 and 5 percent. The cost of the item is MOST NEARLY
    A. $5.50   B. $6.00   C. $8.50   D. $9.00

27. Assuming that it requires 6 man-days to replace a sidewalk 4 feet wide x 120 feet long, then a similar sidewalk 8 feet wide x 78 feet long would require MOST NEARLY _____ man-days.
    A. 6   B. 8   C. 10   D. 14

28. The initials S.S., as used in connection with window glass, means
    A. single strength
    B. single silicon
    C. sharp section
    D. striated surface

29. If a screwed galvanized iron fitting is used in a copper or brass line, the MOST probable result would be that the
    A. galvanized iron fitting will rust quickly
    B. brass line will have to be replaced
    C. galvanized fitting will outlast the brass line
    D. brass line will corrode

30. A plumbing sketch is drawn to a scale of 1/8" = 1 foot. A horizontal water line measuring 6 3/4" on the sketch would be equivalent to _____ feet of water pipe.
    A. 27   B. 41   C. 54   D. 64

31. The tool that holds the die when threading a 2" pipe is called a
    A. yoke
    B. punch
    C. vise
    D. stock

32. Of the following, the BEST fastener to use in a hollow wall is the _____ bolt.
    A. expansion
    B. carriage
    C. machine nut and
    D. toggle

33. A 5 hp, 3 phase, 208-volt squirrel cage motor is USUALLY started by means of a(n)
    A. compensator
    B. across the line starter
    C. reduced voltage starter
    D. 3 point starting box

34. When using a voltmeter in testing an electric circuit, the voltmeter should be connected
    A. across the circuit
    B. in series with the circuit
    C. in parallel or series with the circuit
    D. in series with the active element

35. The coloring material in an exterior wall paint is called the
    A. solvent
    B. lacquer
    C. vehicle
    D. pigment

KEY (CORRECT ANSWERS)

1. C	11. A	21. B	31. D
2. A	12. D	22. C	32. D
3. D	13. B	23. D	33. B
4. A	14. D	24. A	34. A
5. D	15. C	25. B	35. D
6. A	16. B	26. D	
7. B	17. C	27. B	
8. C	18. B	28. A	
9. C	19. C	29. A	
10. B	20. D	30. C	

TEST 2

DIRECTIONS: Each question or incomplete statement is followed by several suggested answers or completions. Select the one that BEST answers the question or completes the statement. *PRINT THE LETTER OF THE CORRECT ANSWER IN THE SPACE AT THE RIGHT.*

1. The refrigerant MOST often used in household refrigerators is
   A. argon
   B. lithium bromide
   C. ammonia
   D. freon-12

   1._____

2. When tie or identical low bids are submitted for a competitive contract under $1,000 by two bidders, the successful bidder may be selected by
   A. requesting a new bid from a third party
   B. tossing a coin
   C. drawing lots
   D. requesting new bids from all the bidders and selecting the lowest bid

   2._____

3. The one of the following which is LEAST important in developing a budget for the next fiscal year for project maintenance is the
   A. adequacy of the current year's budget
   B. changes in workload that can be anticipated
   C. budget restrictions indicated in a memorandum covering budget preparations
   D. staff reassignments which are expected during the next fiscal year

   3._____

4. The LEAST likely subject to be discussed at a planning meeting with assistant superintendents and foremen is the
   A. allocation of responsibility for the phases of administration
   B. provision for coordination and follow-up
   C. setting goals for each supervisor's section
   D. assignment of tasks to individual workers

   4._____

5. From the standpoint of equal opportunity, the MOST critical item that a superintendent should focus on is
   A. assigning only minority workers to supervisory positions
   B. helping minority employees to upgrade their knowledge so they may qualify for higher positions
   C. placing minority workers in job categories above their present level of ability so that they can "sink" or "swim"
   D. disregarding merit system principles

   5._____

6. After careful deliberation, you have decided that one of your workers should be disciplined. It is MOST important that the
   A. discipline be severe for best results
   B. discipline be delayed as long as possible
   C. worker understands why he is being disciplined
   D. other workers be consulted before the discipline is administered

   6._____

7. Of the following, the MOST important qualities of an employee chosen for a supervisory position are
    A. education and intelligence
    B. interest in the objectives and activities of the agency
    C. skill in performing the type of work to be supervised
    D. knowledge of the work and leadership ability

8. A tenant complains to you that he was wet by the spray from a garden hose handled carelessly by one of your workers and that he can identify the worker. The BEST course of action is for you to
    A. express regret and assure the tenant that you will caution the worker
    B. try to convince the tenant that he did not get too wet
    C. assure the tenant that charges will be preferred against the worker
    D. arrange a meeting between tenant and worker and make the worker apologize

9. In preparing a report to his supervisor, a superintendent should
    A. include irrelevant matters to show a greater grasp of the problem
    B. not allow anyone to read and criticize the draft of the report for fear that he will seem incompetent
    C. prepare an outline before writing the draft of the report
    D. always question whether or not the report is necessary

10. A superintendent who is preparing a report on a study which was requested by his supervisor should make the FIRST section of the report a discussion of the
    A. situation which exists currently
    B. method of instituting the recommendations
    C. objections to the report
    D. additional equipment needed to carry out the recommendations

11. A superintendent should read the work orders for the maintenance men each morning so that
    A. every work order is completed the day it is received
    B. all work orders are handled in chronological order regardless of the kind of work involved
    C. the work which the maintenance men do not like to do is not postponed continually
    D. the maintenance men know that you are checking up on them every minute of the day

12. MOST tenants in a housing project will
    A. separate in their minds the actions of a superintendent and the policies of the housing authority
    B. consider what the superintendent does as the policy of the housing authority
    C. realize that superintendents will follow policies that are undesirable to the housing authority
    D. make allowances for the policies a superintendent follows

13. Mortar joints in old brickwork are BEST repaired by
    A. setting
    B. framing
    C. taping
    D. pointing

14. An equipment rental allowance includes the rental charge plus 9%. If a piece of equipment is rented for 11 days at $36 per day, the total equipment allowance is MOST NEARLY
    A. $360   B. $390   C. $420   D. $450

15. The extinguishing agent in a soda-acid fire extinguisher is
    A. water
    B. hydrochloric acid
    C. sodium bicarbonate
    D. carbon dioxide

16. A building heated by an oil-fired boiler used 3,500 gallons of oil during a period of 2100 degree days. The number of gallons of oil that probably would be burned by the same building over a period of 1800 degree days is
    A. 2700   B. 3000   C. 3400   D. 3700

17. Of the following, the BEST chemical to use to melt ice on pavements is
    A. carbon tetrachloride
    B. calcium chloride
    C. potassium hydroxide
    D. sodium fluoride

18. The MAIN purpose of periodic inspection and tests of electrical equipment is to
    A. encourage workers to take better care of the equipment
    B. familiarize the workers with the equipment
    C. keep the workers busy during otherwise slack periods
    D. discover minor faults before they develop into major faults

19. The greatest benefit of job evaluation is in
    A. placing the blame for inefficiency
    B. testing the intelligence of custodial workers
    C. eliminating duplication of activities
    D. determining efficiency ratings

20. The current rating of the fuse to use in a lighting circuit is determined by the
    A. connected load
    B. line voltage
    C. capacity of the wiring
    D. rating of the switch

21. Portable fire extinguishers which are suitable for Class C fires should be identified by the letter C inside a
    A. triangle
    B. circle
    C. square
    D. five-point star

22. In the piping system for domestic gas supply,
    A. risers must have a drip leg and cap at the bottom
    B. gasketed unions are used to join pipes
    C. couplings with running threads are used to join pipes
    D. composition disc globe valves are used to throttle the gas

23. A cast iron soil pipe-bend having an angle of 45 degrees is COMMONLY called a _____ bend.
    A. 1/16   B. 1/8   C. 1/4   D. return

24. Of the following, the LEAST likely cause of faulty atomization of fuel oil in a rotary cup oil burner is
    A. too low an oil temperature
    B. too low an oil pressure
    C. insufficient secondary air
    D. insufficient primary air

25. In order to minimize the labor involved in replacing an electric motor, which is directly connected to a centrifugal house pump, the specification for the new motor should include the
    A. shaft size
    B. NEMA frame size
    C. end bell size
    D. NEMA design letter

26. The supervisor of a large group of maintenance workers will most likely find that the GREATEST number of them will be motivated by
    A. letting them plan and control their own work
    B. giving them more responsibility
    C. supervising them very closely
    D. considering each of them individually and treating them accordingly

27. An example of a non-flammable liquid is
    A. floor sealer
    B. kerosene
    C. carbon tetrachloride
    D. benzene

28. Which of the following malfunctions is MOST hazardous to life? 28.____
    A. Short circuit in an outlet box
    B. Gas leak from a stove connection
    C. Water leak behind a kitchen sink
    D. Steam leak from a stop valve

29. A supervisor observes that there is a constant backlog of work tickets, 29.____
    which results in a long delay between the time when a complaint is
    reported by a tenant and when the work is completed.
    In handling this situation, the supervisor should
    A. ignore the situation if he is certain he can avoid being blamed for it
    B. ignore the situation because it is really the responsibility of the
       superintendent
    C. explain the situation to the superintendent and recommend waiting
       until the situation gets so bad that the central office will realize that
       more permanent maintenance men are needed
    D. explain the situation to the superintendent and recommend that he
       request the loan of several maintenance men from the central
       office for sufficient time to reduce the backlog to normal

30. A supervisor assigns a maintenance man to do an emergency job and 30.____
    gives him the authority to obtain the help and equipment he needs to
    complete the job.
    Under these circumstances, FINAL responsibility for the job
    A. belongs to the maintenance man
    B. remains with the supervisor
    C. cannot be determined
    D. is shared between the maintenance man and the supervisor

KEY (CORRECT ANSWERS)

1. D	11. C	21. B
2. C	12. B	22. A
3. D	13. D	23. B
4. D	14. C	24. C
5. B	15. A	25. B
6. C	16. B	26. D
7. D	17. B	27. C
8. A	18. D	28. B
9. C	19. C	29. D
10. A	20. C	30. B

EXAMINATION SECTION
TEST 1

DIRECTIONS: Each question or incomplete statement is followed by several suggested answers or completions. Select the one that BEST answers the question or completes the statement. *PRINT THE LETTER OF THE CORRECT ANSWER IN THE SPACE AT THE RIGHT.*

1. An instrument that is USUALLY mounted on a boiler control panel and which is read in inches of water is known as a(n) _____ gauge.

    A. pressure
    B. draft
    C. stack temperature
    D. Orsat indicator

2. The type of pump which should be used to supply fuel oil to a low-pressure boiler is the _____ pump.

    A. centrifugal
    B. diaphragm
    C. rotary gear
    D. reciprocating

3. A thermostatic radiator trap which is working satisfactorily will

    A. *open* to pass the steam
    B. *open* to pass the condensate
    C. *close* to retain the cool air
    D. *close* to retain the condensate

4. Readings of stack temperature and percentage of carbon dioxide are useful in the boiler room in determining changes in the boiler's _____ efficiency.

    A. mechanical
    B. volumetric
    C. overall
    D. combustion

5. In the start-up cycle of a boiler which is equipped with all of the following devices, the device that should be energized BEFORE all the others is the

    A. magnetic oil valve
    B. ignition transformer
    C. gas solenoid valve
    D. fresh air louvre motor

6. The one of the following valves which is electrically operated is the _____ valve.

    A. pressure relief
    B. magnetic oil
    C. check
    D. thermostatic control

7. In an installation where there is only one fuel-oil pump set, a duplex strainer is PREFERABLY used because

    A. one side of the strainer can be cleaned without interrupting the flow of oil
    B. one side of the strainer will screen out much finer particles than the other side
    C. the flow of oil can be directed through both sides at the same time, thereby increasing the velocity of the oil
    D. cleaning of a duplex strainer is not required during the heating season

8. A higher-than-normal vacuum reading on a gauge which is attached to the suction side of a fuel-oil pump generally indicates that there is

    A. no oil in the tank
    B. a clogged strainer in the suction line
    C. a broken fitting in the suction line
    D. worn packing on the pump

9. The one of the following which is NOT a possible point of entry of water leaking into the fuel-oil storage tank is the

   A. fuel fill pipe can
   B. sounding well plug
   C. steam coil in a fuel-oil heater
   D. fire box side of the furnace wall

10. When an air vaporstat which is connected to an automatic rotary cup oil burner senses the loss of primary air pressure in the fan housing, it *de-energizes* the

    A. burner motor-starter coil
    B. magnetic-oil valve
    C. secondary air-damper control
    D. modutrol motor

11. A steam boiler which is externally fired and in which the hot gases pass through the tubes is commonly known as a _____ boiler.

    A. Scotch
    B. locomotive
    C. horizontal return tubular
    D. vertical tubular

12. The modulating pressuretrol on an automatic rotary cup oil-fired boiler controls the

    A. modutrol motor circuit
    B. magnetic oil valve
    C. burner motor starter
    D. electric heater

13. The reason for *blowing down* a boiler is to

    A. *lower* the boiler water level below the boiler tubes
    B. *reduce* the concentration of dissolved solids in the boiler water
    C. *reduce* the concentration of dissolved oxygen in the boiler water
    D. *eliminate* the need for treating the boiler water chemically

14. The one of the following boiler pressure-actuated devices which should be adjusted to operate at the highest pre-sure setting is the

    A. pop-safety valve
    B. manual-reset pressuretrol
    C. modulating pressuretrol
    D. limit pressuretrol

15. The BEST procedure for testing the operation of a low-water cutout is to *lower* the _____ until the burner shuts off.

    A. boiler water level *rapidly*
    B. boiler water level *slowly*
    C. water level in the water column *rapidly*
    D. water level in the water column *slowly*

16. If the water disappears from the gauge glass on a low-pressure oil-fired boiler, the FIRST action the boiler operator should take is to

    A. shut off the water
    B. add water to the boiler until the glass fills up to the correct level
    C. open the bottom blow-down valve
    D. blow down the water column

17. On a certain day, the lowest outside temperature was 20° F and the highest was 40° F. The number of degree days for this day is

    A. 25   B. 30   C. 35   D. 45

18. A vacuum return line pump should NOT be operated with the electrical control set for

    A. continuous operation   B. float and vacuum control
    C. float control only   D. vacuum control only

19. The PREFERRED location for a Dunham Selector is on the _____ exposure of the building.

    A. north   B. east   C. south   D. west

20. Maintaining a Dunham Heat Balancer in good working order requires *annual* cleaning of its

    A. radiator fins   B. relay contacts
    C. solenoid valve   D. fulcrum

21. A chemical useful in reducing the concentration of oxygen in boiler water is

    A. tannin   B. amines
    C. sodium sulphite   D. sodium carbonate

22. Smoke alarms which must be installed on oil-fired boilers should create a loud signal and a red flashing light upon the emission of an air contaminant whose density, when compared to the standard smoke chart, appears darker than Number _____ on the chart.

    A. 1   B. 2   C. 3   D. 4

23. Samples for the testing of boiler water should be taken from the

    A. bottom blow-off   B. condensate tank
    C. water column   D. condensate-return line

24. In a building which is heated by an oil-fired boiler, 2,100 gallons of fuel oil were burned in a period in which the degree days reached a total of 1,400.
    If all other conditions remained constant, the number of gallons of fuel oil that would be burned in this building during a period in which the degree days reached a total of 3,600 is

    A. 2,400   B. 2,900   C. 4,800   D. 5,400

25. Of the following fuels, the one with the HIGHEST viscosity is

    A. kerosene   B. natural gas   C. #6 oil   D. #2 oil

4 (#1)

KEY (CORRECT ANSWERS)

1.	B	11.	C
2.	C	12.	A
3.	B	13.	B
4.	D	14.	A
5.	D	15.	B
6.	B	16.	A
7.	A	17.	C
8.	B	18.	D
9.	D	19.	A
10.	B	20.	A

21. C
22. A
23. C
24. D
25. C

TEST 2

DIRECTIONS: Each question or incomplete statement is followed by several suggested answers or completions. Select the one that BEST answers the question or completes the statement. *PRINT THE LETTER OF THE CORRECT ANSWER IN THE SPACE AT THE RIGHT.*

1. The device which **protects** the boiler from damage due to low water is the

    A. fusible plug
    B. fusible link
    C. vaporstat
    D. aquastat

2. In a low-pressure fire-tube boiler, the oil burner should be shut off BEFORE

    A. operating the soot blower
    B. taking a flue gas sample
    C. blowing down the boiler
    D. blowing down the water column

3. A domestic hot water circulating pump is started and stopped automatically by means of a(n) _____ in the line.

    A. pressuretrol; supply
    B. pressuretrol; return
    C. aquastat; supply
    D. aquastat; return

4. On a steam-heated domestic hot water generator, the device which acts to *prevent* damage to the coils due to a high internal pressure differential between the coil and the tank is the

    A. pressure relief valve
    B. vacuum breaker
    C. air vent valve
    D. steam trap

5. In the city, the rules and regulations concerning the cleaning of a water tank which is part of a building's domestic water supply are specified by the

    A. fire department
    B. department of housing and buildings
    C. city sanitary code
    D. board of water supply

6. A housing fireman, making a preliminary inspection of a fuel oil delivery truck, discovers that the level of the oil in one compartment is far below the marker.
   In this case, he SHOULD

    A. reject the shipment and order that it be returned to the terminal
    B. measure the level of the oil in the low compartment by *sticking* and report his findings to the superintendent before unloading
    C. read the liquidometer gauge before allowing the truck to be unloaded and again after it has been unloaded and record the difference in gallons to determine the amount for which payment should be made
    D. ignore the low level if it is in only one compartment

7. Of the following fire extinguishers, the one which should be provided for use in the elevator machine room is the _____ type.

    A. carbon dioxide
    B. soda-acid
    C. foam
    D. loaded-stream

8. The wall surface which does NOT have to be washed from the bottom up to avoid streaking is a(n) _____ wall.

    A. semi-gloss painted
    B. enamel painted
    C. glazed tile
    D. unglazed tile

9. The one of the following practices which is GENERALLY recommended to prolong the useful life of a corn broom is

    A. soaking a new broom overnight before using it for the first time to remove brittleness
    B. storing the broom with the tips of the straws resting on the floor to keep the edges even
    C. keeping the straws moistened when sweeping
    D. storing the broom in a warm humid enclosure to prevent drying of the bristles

10. While a caretaker is sweeping the public corridors and stairways, he notices some crayon marks on walls and stains on the floors.
    He SHOULD

    A. stop sweeping and remove the stains immediately
    B. finish sweeping and then return to remove the stains
    C. make note of the marks and stains in his building and remove them once a month
    D. make a note of the marks and stains and report them to the superintendent so that the cause can be eliminated before the stains are removed

11. When transporting the equipment required for mopping stairhalls and corridors, a caretaker should NOT

    A. attempt to do it alone
    B. carry water in the pails because spillage may cause a tenant to slip and fall
    C. use the elevator
    D. carry the equipment in both hands when climbing stairs

12. A caretaker should apply washing solution to a portion of a painted wall and should rinse the same area before applying the solution to another area.
    In order to allow sufficient time for the solution to take effect on the soil, the area covered each time should be APPROXIMATELY _____ square feet.

    A. 20
    B. 60
    C. 160
    D. 600

13. Asphalt tile floors should be maintained by coating them with

    A. water emulsion wax
    B. paste wax
    C. oil emulsion wax
    D. neat's-foot oil

14. The broom with which a caretaker should sweep an asphalt-paved playground is the _____ broom.

    A. hair
    B. corn
    C. garage
    D. Scotch

15. A paper sticker should be used by a caretaker to

    A. pick up litter and fruit skins
    B. make temporary warning signs to be placed around wet floor areas
    C. indicate on the elevator panel on which floor he is working
    D. feed old newspapers into the incinerator

16. The type of floor which should be cleaned by sweeping and then mopping with an abrasive detergent is the _____ floor.

    A. painted cement
    B. unpainted cement
    C. asphalt tile
    D. terrazzo

17. The term *cutting the water* refers to one step in the procedure for

    A. cleaning windows
    B. treating boiler water
    C. watering lawns
    D. washing walls

18. Stains on ceramic tile may be removed by very carefully using a dilute solution of _____ acid.

    A. acetic
    B. oxalic
    C. sulphuric
    D. hydrochloric

19. The directions on the label of a bottle of detergent call for mixing four ounces of detergent with one gallon of water to make a cleaning solution for washing floors.
    In order to obtain a LARGER amount of solution of the same strength, one quart of the detergent should be mixed with _____ gallons of water.

    A. 2   B. 4   C. 6   D. 8

20. Garden soil which has a pH reading of 6.0 is said to be

    A. neutral
    B. slightly acid
    C. slightly alkaline
    D. strongly acid

21. Acid soil can be treated so that the acidity is reduced by using

    A. limestone
    B. peat moss
    C. humus
    D. nitrogen

22. The one of the following procedures which is NOT recommended for growing turfgrass in shaded areas is to

    A. fertilize more frequently than normal
    B. water deeply and frequently
    C. compact the soil as much as possible
    D. prune shallow tree roots as much as possible

23. Hedges should be trimmed so that the top is _____ than the bottom with the solid leaf growth starting _____ the ground.

    A. *narrower;* about eighteen inches above
    B. *narrower;* as close as possible to
    C. *wider;* about eighteen inches above
    D. *wider;* as close as possible to

24. A checklist of outdoor tasks which should be performed in March and April should NOT include

   A. fertilizing lawn areas
   B. applying dormant spray
   C. cleaning window wells
   D. spraying broad-leaved weeds

25. Lawns should be mowed when the grass has attained a height of _____ inch(es) with the mower set at _____ inch(es).

   A. 4; 3   B. 3; 2   C. 2; 1   D. 1; 1/2

KEY (CORRECT ANSWERS)

1. A
2. C
3. D
4. B
5. C

6. B
7. A
8. C
9. A
10. B

11. D
12. C
13. A
14. C
15. A

16. B
17. A
18. D
19. D
20. B

21. A
22. C
23. B
24. D
25. B

TEST 3

DIRECTIONS: Each question or incomplete statement is followed by several suggested answers or completions. Select the one that BEST answers the question or completes the statement. *PRINT THE LETTER OF THE CORRECT ANSWER IN THE SPACE AT THE RIGHT.*

1. The number of employees required for raising the national flag in the morning and lowering it at night is:
   _____ employee(s) to raise; _____ employee(s) to lower and fold it.

   A. One; one B. One; two C. Two; two D. Two; one

   1.____

2. The component of fertilizers which aids in keeping grass from turning brown in the summer time is

   A. limestone B. calcium C. chlordane D. nitrogen

   2.____

3. The one of the following chemicals which can be used to melt ice on sidewalks is

   A. carbon tetrachloride B. methane
   C. acetic acid D. sodium chloride

   3.____

4. A snow fence, which is used to prevent the drifting of snow over certain areas, is USUALLY made of

   A. wood slats wired together
   B. plastic-coated woven wire
   C. compacted snow
   D. two horizontal wood rails joining vertical posts

   4.____

5. The area of a lawn which is 58 feet wide by 96 feet long is MOST NEARLY _____ square feet.

   A. 5000 B. 5500 C. 6000 D. 6500

   5.____

6. All elevators must be inspected by the department of

   A. buildings B. air resources
   C. health D. labor

   6.____

7. The training of personnel in the procedure for restoring stalled elevators to service and releasing passengers from stalled elevators should be given by the

   A. project superintendent
   B. chief superintendent
   C. project elevator mechanic
   D. project assistant superintendent

   7.____

8. When a maintenance man is greasing a ball bearing pillow block which is equipped with shaft seals, he should pump grease through the grease fitting UNTIL

   A. a strong back pressure is felt on the gun
   B. grease starts to leak past both seals
   C. clean grease starts to leak out of the opened drain hole
   D. six strokes of the gun handle are counted

   8.____

9. In buildings, safety checks of every elevator hatch door should be made each day by the

   A. caretaker
   B. elevator mechanic
   C. assistant superintendent
   D. maintenance man

10. The BEST way to find a Freon 12 refrigerant leak in a domestic refrigerator is by using a

    A. sulphur match
    B. plumber's candle
    C. peroxide bath
    D. halide torch

11. Good preventive maintenance of mechanical equipment in a housing project should result in an INCREASE in the

    A. frequency of unscheduled repairs
    B. overall cost of maintenance
    C. down-time of the equipment
    D. efficiency of service

12. In a building, plexiglass can be used to replace ordinary glass which is located in

    A. apartments that are more than 150 feet above curb level
    B. stairhalls
    C. front entrance doors
    D. fire-resistive opening protective assemblies

13. The BEST bit to use in an electric drill when drilling a hole in masonry is a(n)

    A. high-speed steel bit
    B. auger
    C. carbide-tipped bit
    D. tapered-shank tool steel bit

14. The type of fastener used to attach a butt hinge to a metal door is a

    A. round head rivet
    B. flat head machine screw
    C. filister head cap screw
    D. flat head wood screw

15. Burner gas cocks on kitchen stoves should be lubricated when necessary with

    A. refrigerant oil
    B. graphited grease
    C. penetrating oil
    D. cutting oil

16. A type of portable tool used to bend electrical conduit is called a

    A. helve   B. newel   C. spandrel   D. hickey

17. A device used to guide a handsaw to cut boards at a desired angle to form an evenly divided angle joint is called a

    A. miter box   B. backsaw   C. try square   D. protractor

18. The criteria governing preventive maintenance of vehicles require that all of the following be done at certain intervals.
    The one which must be done MOST frequently is

    A. changing the engine oil
    B. changing the engine oil filter
    C. checking the radiator coolant level
    D. rotating the tires

19. Only the plug on the electric cord of a refrigerator gets very hot when the refrigerator is operating normally. The MOST likely cause of this is that there is a(n)   19.____

    A. poor electrical connection in the plug
    B. oversized fuse in the circuit
    C. short circuit in the plug
    D. short circuit in the motor

20. Of two back-to-back plumbing fixtures are stopped up at the same time, the stoppage is MOST likely in the   20.____

    A. trap of one of the fixtures
    B. waste line in the wall
    C. vent line in the wall
    D. vacuum breaker

21. The procedure which should be followed to stop a faucet drip in a faucet which is equipped with non-renewable seats is to replace   21.____

    A. the faucet with a new one
    B. all the washers and seats with new ones
    C. all the washers with new ones and grind the seats until smooth
    D. both spindles

22. The ADVANTAGE of using a flexible coupling over using a rigid coupling on the shaft of a house pump is that the flexible coupling   22.____

    A. allows for slight misalignment of the shafts
    B. can transmit more power than a rigid coupling
    C. provides a cushioned start
    D. prevents overloading of the motor

23. The one of the following attitudes which a good supervisor should encourage among his subordinates is that they   23.____

    A. should want to do the best possible job
    B. should work only well enough to get by
    C. do not work as hard as the workers in other projects
    D. must produce more work each day than they did on the previous day

24. The supervisory function which deals with the determination of what work a supervisor wants done by his staff is known as   24.____

    A. planning   B. staffing
    C. directing   D. controlling

25. The one of the following personality traits that is UNDESIRABLE is   25.____

    A. self-confidence   B. intelligence
    C. initiative   D. indifference

KEY (CORRECT ANSWERS)

1.	B	11.	D
2.	D	12.	C
3.	D	13.	C
4.	A	14.	B
5.	B	15.	B
6.	A	16.	D
7.	C	17.	A
8.	C	18.	C
9.	A	19.	A
10.	D	20.	B

21. C
22. A
23. A
24. A
25. D

www.ingramcontent.com/pod-product-compliance
Lightning Source LLC
Chambersburg PA
CBHW081834300426
44116CB00014B/2584